THE
SCENE STUDY
BOOK

THE SCENE STUDY BOOK

ROADMAP TO SUCCESS

BRUCE MILLER

AN IMPRINT OF
HAL•LEONARD®

Published in 2010 by Limelight Editions
An Imprint of Hal Leonard Corporation
7777 West Bluemound Road
Milwaukee, WI 53213

Trade Book Division Editorial Offices
19 West 21st Street, New York, NY 10010

Parts of this book first appeared in some form in *Dramatics* magazine and in the journal *Teaching Theatre*.

Grateful acknowledgment is made to Samuel French, Inc. for permission to reprint GO LOOK by Chris Graybill: Copyright © 1995 by Christopher Graybill.

CAUTION: Professionals and amateurs are hereby warned that "GO LOOK" being fully protected under the copyright laws of the United States of America, the British Commonwealth countries, including Canada, and the other countries of the Copyright Union, is subject to a royalty. All rights, including professional, amateur, motion picture, recitation, public reading, radio, television and cable broadcasting, and the rights of translation into foreign languages, are strictly reserved. Any inquiry regarding the availability of performance rights, or the purchase of individual copies of the authorized acting edition, must be directed to Samuel French Inc., 45 West 25 Street, NY, NY 10010 with other locations in Hollywood.

Printed in the United States of America
Book design by Kristina Rolander

Library of Congress Cataloging-in-Publication Data

Miller, Bruce J.
  The scene study book : roadmap to success / Bruce J. Miller.
    p. cm.
  Includes bibliographical references.
  ISBN 978-0-87910-371-2 (pbk.)
  1. Acting--Handbooks, manuals, etc. I. Title.
  PN2061.M4655 2010
  792.02'8071--dc22
                                        2009052716
  ISBN 978-0-87910-371-2

www.limelighteditions.com

TO MY STUDENTS —
WHO TAUGHT ME EVERYTHING

CONTENTS

INTRODUCTION

Definition of good acting: *acting that is believable while telling the best possible story that serves the script.*

Whether you're a serious high school actor or thinking about acting as a profession, your primary focus should be on learning how to do it efficiently and well. As you study your craft, you'll need to master the skills that will get you the job and help you do it effectively once you get it. It is not unreasonable to assume that the majority of the work you will do in the future will be based on scripted material. That's how most plays and movies are done. Improvisation and theatre games are all well and good, but being able to perform exercises or create imaginative improvisational work seldom translates directly into being able to work from a script effectively. That means that the analysis and synthesis skills you learn are essential to your survival and success.

But other aspects of your work are equally essential. Good actors must be able to take what they have gleaned from their analysis and translate it into actions—actions that can be played believably on the stage. Actors must be able to make physical choices that not only further the story moment by moment, but do so in a way that is clear and compelling to the audience. These choices must also, whenever possible, reveal the character's thoughts and feelings while being consistent with the script provided by the playwright.

Finally, good actors must be able to take what they have distilled from analysis, converted to actions, and developed in rehearsal to the point where they no longer have to think about it. Ultimately, they must be able to trust that what they learned in rehearsal is in their muscles and brains and hearts, so they can forget about it and listen and react moment to moment on the stage as though they were hearing the words and seeing what's going on around them for the first time.

No acting exercise or series of exercises can incorporate or embrace the necessities of this kind of acting better than a scene study class. Everything you will have to do as an actor playing from a script is included in the scene study process—from analysis to playing actions, both physical (what you physically do) and psychological (going after what you need). Acting exercises and theatre games are simulations only. They are no more like the acting you do onstage or on-screen than Madden Football is like playing a game in the NFL. Madden Football may be fun to play, but it is a distant second to actually doing it. Acting games and exercises, like computer football, are no doubt fun and may be instructional, but they have no direct bearing on what you will do when the ball is metaphorically handed off to you. That is why, for most actors, the scene study class is something they do over and over again. It teaches them the skills they need and sharpens the skills they already possess. Good actors may change teachers time and again, but it is almost always the scene study format that acting teachers will use to develop their student actors' skills.

Actors who work with scripted material need to be able to do the following:

- Find the story being told and figure out their part in the telling of it
- Make physical and psychological choices that are clear and compelling and that serve the script
- Use the dialogue believably and effectively
- Listen and react onstage, making adjustments as needed to the here and now

In the book you are about to read, all of these issues will be addressed by taking you through the scene study process, from selecting a scene and a partner, to analyzing and scoring a scene, through the blocking and fine tuning of the work. You'll learn what you should expect from yourself, from your teacher, and from the material you are working on. You will get ideas on everything from how to find good material that will serve you to how to work with even the most difficult partner. This book covers the essentials of scene study in such a way that you will not waste your precious time by doing things that won't serve you or your development as an actor. The first chapters deal with the practical reading and interpreting of a script. The remainder of the book deals with the actual step-by-step process involved in scene study. Hopefully, you will find the approach to acting in this book to be simple, direct, and practical. It will fit into any technique you are currently using or will learn in the future. In short, there is no other book on acting like this one. My hope is that you will find it as valuable as I think it is.

Notes: The approach you will find in this book is action-based, or external, in its approach. It does not rely on emotional truth as its source for choice making; it relies instead on executing actions. Anyone can execute believable actions; not everyone can connect believably and consistently with their inner resources. Obviously, there is a place for exploring the inner self in acting training. It often makes the difference between good acting and great acting. Nonetheless, I have chosen to focus on actions in this book, because all actors with dedication and commitment to craft can master the basics of action-based acting and provide themselves with a solid foundation that can be built on with other techniques. Besides, executing a committed action often results in an emotional reaction, simply because humans are wired that way. Just punch a wall with commitment and you'll know what I'm talking about.

If any of the vocabulary you find here is foreign to you, just consult the glossary in the back of the book. It will help you avoid getting confused.

As you can see in the table of contents, the book is divided into two sections—the first section on analysis and the second section on the scene study class specifically. All scene study requires analysis before your work with a partner should begin. This is homework and should be done independently, but it is a vital part of any solid craft and certainly a vital element in the scene study process. For that reason I have made it a prominent part of the book, and it should be taken very seriously if you are a serious acting student. However, you will find that most, if not all, of the chapters in this book can be read independently. That means if you are not a beginner, you may want to jump around to review particular chapters or to refresh a particular aspect of your craft.

PART 1
ANALYSIS

CHAPTER ONE

THINKING AS A STORYTELLER

WHY DO SO MANY ACTORS ASSUME THAT SINCE THEY know what the concept of playing an action is, they will automatically be able to pick actions that will work in the play or scene they are rehearsing? Why do they assume that if they read the entire play, they will automatically know what is most useful to them as actors? Why do they assume that simply because they have read the play, they have absorbed the sequence of events that we call the plot of a story? All of this takes practice and persistence. It cannot be learned overnight. Yet practical analysis is probably the area of acting on which actors spend the least amount of time.

Remember, drama is primarily about action, not emotion. And the characters you play do not exist outside the pages of the script they spring from. Therefore, any allegiance to character rather than to the story contained in the script is probably a misguided loyalty. It is first and foremost your obligation to help tell the playwright's story rather than your character's. That means you have to understand the mechanics of the script provided by the playwright and, from that, make your own storytelling contribution before you engage in any practical scene work. Take a moment and examine the list of bullet points below. Each, I believe, is a principle that you must bring to any script you are about to work on. See if you agree.

- Characters are most effectively created by playing their actions rather than their emotions.
- Those actions are suggested by the script that those characters serve.
- By approaching your work in this manner, the script can help you do clearer, more exciting, and more believable work than when you consider the script as only a servant to your own individual creative efforts.

Before proceeding any further, there is another important concept worth mentioning—a point that probably needs to be emphasized strongly and clearly. Here it is: Reading a play for a theatrical production or scene work requires a very different focus than when you read a play for an English class. The parts of a play your literature teacher asked you to focus on are probably the things least useful to you as an actor. Conversely, the things you most took for granted when you read or studied a play as literature probably make up the heart of its dramatic arc or throughline.

The plot of a play, for instance, seems ridiculously obvious—it happens before our eyes and we can take it in without thinking about it. As a student in English class, you might even remember being insulted when that mediocre teacher asked you only plot questions on an exam. Yet when you are asked as an actor to talk about the specifics of plot, you may often find it difficult to do so. Though it might seem elementary, it can be hard for you to list the important events in a play one by one sequentially. You may be at a loss if asked to describe how each event was triggered by the one that preceded it. But this seemingly simplistic task is the very essence of what is required to tell a story onstage clearly and fully. If you doubt what I'm saying, think back to a movie or TV show you saw recently and try sequencing the plot events chronologically in a cause-and-effect manner.

If you found that exercise harder than you anticipated, you probably now realize that you need to put a lot more effort into your analysis skills. You might also realize that the connection between your analysis and what you choose to do onstage is far more important to your ultimate success as an actor than you had previously thought. Only by going through a process of investigation many, many times will you begin to develop the habit of approaching a script by reading actively and by asking the right questions. It may take years to fully develop a set of reliable skills, but the investment will be well worth it. You must read as many plays as you can, and read each one actively—read by continually asking questions about why the playwright wrote what he wrote. This is one of the most important acting disciplines and skills you can give yourself. The fact is that if you are going to be a good actor, there is a lot of homework involved. The sooner you commit to that, the better.

As you begin to develop your script analysis skills, it is essential that you keep in mind at all times that playwrights write plays with the intention of telling a good story. If a play keeps getting published and performed, chances are there's a good story there, even if you don't see it at the beginning of your analysis. If you really want to become a good actor, one who can work independently, it is your job to learn how to find that good story. Only by recognizing that story and by isolating its components will you later be able to build a dramatic performance moment by moment, beat by beat, and scene by scene. You must accept the fact that well-selected and well-thought-out choices based on the script will increase the believability of your work, as well as improve your work's clarity and dramatic potential. These choices can be made only if you understand how the script works.

CHAPTER

FINDING THE STORY AND PLAYING IT

ACTORS AND PLAYWRIGHTS HAVE MORE IN COMMON than one might think. Both are charged with telling the story of the script. In the case of the playwright, the charge is a creative one. In the case of the actor, it is more interpretive. But the fact is, both playwrights and actors have to get the story right, or the play or production is just not going to work. If your work is going to be successful, you will have to concern yourself with analysis as much as action. Put simply, you must be able to choose the right action before doing it. The wrong action, no matter how well executed, can lead the story in the wrong direction and destroy what the playwright has worked so hard to create. The right choice, well executed, can and surely will enhance what the playwright has provided.

Keep in mind that *conflict,* the engine of drama, and the playing of *objectives,* one of the most important tools an actor uses, are strongly interconnected. Playwrights know that conflict is what makes a story run, and actors must find the conflict in the story they are telling before they can determine the objectives they must play—objectives that arise from the conflict in the story. Since actors play their characters' objectives (what the characters need) at every moment, it stands to reason that actors had better choose the right ones. You must teach yourself to view a script in these terms if you hope to develop a craft that will allow you to make and execute choices that tell the story clearly and compellingly.

So let's see how much you know about stories and their construction. Here's a little quiz to test you on the storytelling craft you've put together from your accumulated reading and experience as an actor. The scenario for consideration is as follows:

You're involved in an independent film production of *H.D.: The Great Fall.* The money's raised, the crew's in place, but all the director has to work with is the scenario that raised the money in the first place. The director tells the cast to *make it happen.* "We'll shoot improvisationally," he says, "like an Altman film or like *Curb Your Enthusiasm.*" The scenario he's working from reads as follows:

Humpty Dumpty sat on a wall
Humpty Dumpty had a great fall.
And all the king's horses
And all the king's men
Couldn't put Humpty together again.

So, whaddaya do?

This is where *craft* comes in. Craft is a set of tools that gives you a process to go through that will reliably take you to good acting. At the beginning of this book, I offered up a working definition of good acting. Here it is again in neon. It is a definition that can become a part of your craft tool bag. Any time you're in an acting situation, you can recite this definition and get clues as to how to proceed.

Good acting is acting that is believable, tells the best possible story, and serves the script.

Let's start with the term *believable.* Note that *believable* is not synonymous with "realistic." Realistic, for instance, does not work with all material. The world of a Will Ferrell movie is not realistic. That world is a dumbed-down world, but all the actors as characters buy into it, even when they know that what's going on is too dumb to believe. This allows the audience to buy into it, as well. Shakespeare is not realistic. The language is heightened. Be totally realistic with Shakespeare and you bury the language. You wouldn't want to do that, since the language is the most important element with Shakespeare.

Believability refers more to the style you would use to make the material work, or to put it another way, to create a consistent world for the play or movie to exist in.

So, *H.D.* What is the story? Depends on the world. As you read the scenario, you need to be asking what this world is. Is the world a metaphor, or is it literal? Is it a straight nursery rhyme, or is it a representation of something deeper? In a fully fleshed-out script, you would have to determine the who, what, when, and where (*the given circumstances*) with a careful analysis, looking for clues. But in this case, all we have is the four-line nursery rhyme. Collectively, the production team will have to make the decision about the world of the play and agree to it. Suppose it is agreed that you are going to make this movie literally and let the audience find the metaphor or deeper meaning on their own from what they see. You decide that the where and when of the given circumstances will be Mother Goosey in look and style. But what about the who? Is H.D. a person? If so, what kind? Or is he an egg, as is often portrayed in Mother Goose illustrations? If he is an egg, that would certainly change things about the story being told. This decision, and all the other decisions you make, will strongly affect the story you eventually tell.

All right, what next? Ah, telling the best possible story. (You don't have to worry about serving the script, because there isn't too much hidden in what's provided.) If we break down the story that's provided, we know the following: H.D. on the wall, his falling, his breaking, and the king's men and horses trying and failing to fix him up. If you want to get close up, you might ask why H.D. is referred to in the familiar "Humpty" in the line following "All the king's horses and all the king's men." Did the writer say it that way to elicit sympathy, or was the author making fun of him? How you interpret the line could affect how you portray the story. This is the kind of close work worth doing, by the way, when you're dealing with a good playwright. Everything in a script will be there for a reason. It is your job to determine the reason and then use it.

Some more questions. First of all, is this a story? Answer—not really. Stories have characters who run into a problem, face the problem, and either triumph over the problem or don't. They go on a journey, either literal or metaphorical, and have been changed by that journey by the time the story is over. As was pointed out in the previous chapter, playwrights rely on conflict, the engine of drama, to make stories interesting. Actors must learn to do the same. Conflict comes in three basic flavors:

- Person versus person
- Person versus himself or herself (internal conflict)
- Person versus, nature, society, and so forth

Playwrights, for the most part, rely on person-versus-person or person-versus-self dynamics, but most of the time conflicts end up being person versus person. If two characters are sharing the stage, look for the conflict between them. That's a good basic acting rule to follow.

Once actors find the conflict or conflicts their characters face within the story, they can determine their objectives and play them. The objectives that actors as characters pursue at all times come from this conflict. (Objectives, by the way, are known by many other names depending on the acting teacher or technique. *Intentions, needs, tactics, goals,* and *actions* essentially refer to the same thing.) The next questions regarding the H.D. scenario then become, what are the conflicts that can be mined from this situation, and how do I play them to make a good story? Take a moment and write down all the conflicts you can find that can potentially be mined from the H.D. scenario.

Here's what my list looks like. First, from the potential point of view of H.D. (What kind of conflicts do you find here?):

- Should he go to the wall?
- Should he climb the wall?
- The struggle to get up the wall
- How to handle the danger of sitting on the wall
- How does he get down from the wall?
- Should he get down from the wall?
- Trying to save himself as he falls from the wall

Now from the point of view of the king's men. (What kind of conflicts do you find here?) Note that some of the potential conflicts depend on when they see H.D.—that is, prefall, during fall, or after fall:

- If before fall, how do they try to stop H.D.?
- During fall, what is their reaction? What can and/or should they do, be doing, have done?
- How do they deal with the pieces?
- How do they decide they can't put him together?
- What do they do with the pieces that can't be reassembled?

Now let's take a look at how some of these conflicts work.

Why H.D. should go to the wall and climb it depends on the given circumstances provided by the script, or must be determined by the production team if not provided by the script. Since we have nothing more than the nursery rhyme to go on, we have to make our own decisions. These decisions have to be consistent with the script as it exists, yet they should be choices that make the story as compelling as possible.

If, for instance, we decide that Humpty is a fragile, uncooked and, most importantly, *suicidal* egg, he wants to get atop the wall so that he can do away with himself. He simply *must* find a way to get up that wall to fulfill his objective. This will be difficult. Eggs are not built for climbing. If his overall objective, to kill himself, is strong enough, however, he will make every effort to find a way. His immediate objective, to get up the wall, will be risky and dangerous. And if the king's men—whose policing purposes include keeping the ova population safe—discover him trying to get up that wall, they will do everything in their power to prevent him from committing the action. That will be their immediate objective. The two objectives are clearly in conflict.

If H.D. succeeds in getting up the wall, he will be ready to carry out the next part of his objective or action. Or he might have second thoughts about carrying out his action. The view from that height might weaken his resolve. He might have an internal conflict about carrying out his objective. That doubt will provide a big obstacle to his fulfilling his objective. In the meantime, the king's men will continue to try to stop him—perhaps by changing his mind from below using any and all tactics. Each of these plot devices would work to make the story interesting. Because the actors have been converting conflict into playable actions, a tangible narrative is beginning to unfold.

There are an infinite number of choices available for making any story unfold logically, but each choice must serve to make the story clear, compelling, and consistent with the plot and characters playing them out. These choices must also be consistent with any and all information the playwright has provided. When an actor approaches a script in this manner, he gives himself an entree for making choices that will make him look good, as well as serve the script.

Take a few moments to think about the conflicts you have listed on your own and/or the conflicts I listed here. Try to convert those conflicts into objectives that Humpty and the king's men could be playing. Try to find objectives for each that maintain, as much as possible, a connection between the opposing characters and their needs. You will note that these opposing objectives are invariably interesting. Also note the internal conflicts listed and think through how these internal conflicts can be thought of as objectives with obstacles—obstacles that stand between those chosen objectives and their completion. The bigger the *obstacle,* the bigger the conflict, the better the story. Below you will find an example of what the story hinted at on the previous page is like when further developed or realized.

> Humpty sits atop the wall, exhausted from his climb. As he looks down at the hard ground below, trying to catch his breath, he becomes dizzy. His nausea weakens his resolve. He has thoughts about his happier moments in life. He becomes less sure he wants to jump. Yet he knows he must. He has never carried out anything in his life to fruition. He feels he must do this. It is essential to his broken eggo (pun intended). Back and forth his thoughts go, his internal conflict, an obstacle to carrying out his objective—to end his miserable life. In the meantime, the king's men yell from below, ordering him to stay seated and to wait for them to get to him. They shout up reasons for Humpty not to kill himself. The king's men cajole, flatter, threaten, and warn him. Finally, Humpty jolts himself out of his internal conflict and tries to stand. The wind pushing against him makes this difficult to do, but, faced with his own expectations and the approaching army trying to save him from himself, he overcomes self-doubt, nausea, fear of heights, and even death. Humpty pushes himself to his feet as the king's men continue to shout to him from below and look for ways to get up the wall.

The part of the story recounted above is an exciting one, right? It has life-and-death conflict, strong objectives, lots of risky business, obstacles, and plenty of high-staked physical and psychological action. In short, it has all the elements needed for making good stories and good acting. As an actor who wants to develop a reliable craft, you must learn to think about scripts as puzzles that can be solved through logic and common sense. Here again is the sequence of analysis steps that will make your choices effective and clear.

- Establish the given circumstances
- Determine the conflict
- Convert the conflict into objectives that are as life-and-death as possible
- Make sure these objectives are connected as much as possible to the other characters sharing the stage
- Find and use all obstacles available to ensure that the objectives selected are not easily obtained
- Find physical actions to execute that correspond with the conflict and chosen objectives

Note that actions come in two varieties: physical and psychological. Up to now in this chapter, we have focused mostly on psychological actions—what the characters need or want or, in other words, their objectives. We have learned that strong actions that come from the determined conflict connect the characters onstage and use the conflict—the engine of drama—to make compelling stories. But as the description of the Humpty scenario suggests, *psychological actions* are strongly connected to *physical actions,* as well, and it is often the physical actions that actors playing characters use to communicate thoughts, feelings, and the story.

Remember, actors must be able to physicalize the story being told through their bodies. When an audience watches a play or a movie, they are getting the story through what they see as well as what they hear through dialogue. What characters do and how they do it tells us as much about who they are and what they are all about as does any amount of emoting. An audience cannot read thoughts or feeling. They do not read minds or have the power to peruse the soul or heart. If an audience knows, or thinks they know, what your character is thinking and feeling, either you have told them directly through dialogue (which may not tell the truth—characters lie, you know) or they have inferred it through what you do and the way in which you do it.

Ironically, the physical part of acting is something that too many beginning actors take for granted and, more to the point, simply do not do well. In life we respond to situations automatically. What we do physically is connected, often without any conscious thought, to our brains and emotional systems. If we get angry at someone, our bodies react in a specific way. Our bodies do things. But all too often, when actors hit the stage, their bodies are disconnected from the action. They're so busy thinking about the lines to be said, their choices regarding the script, and their own nerves that their bodies freeze up on them. Two actors standing on the stage nose to nose saying their lines to each other seldom look believable and almost invariably are boring. Yet more often than not, this is what goes down for blocking as I watch a first put-up of a scene in my intermediate acting classes. My students often complain about the flat line delivery of this or that young TV actor they have just seen, but seldom do they complain about those young actors' movement. There is seldom a believability problem when these same actors go from place to place, engage in activity, or communicate with some kind of physical gesture. More to the point, despite the perceived flatness of the lines, these kids are working and making money. They seem to be behaving in a believable manner, and what they do makes sense and adds to the story. Seldom do you see a working actor who can't move. This is too often not the case in acting class.

Here are some examples of what I mean. What would you do with the following lines? Consider each to be a separate scene.

- "I'm leaving, butthead."
- "Give me that candy, right now!"
- "I'll do anything you ask. Anything. Please."
- "Oh, God, I love you, baby!"

Each of these lines implies some kind of strong emotion that is more than likely going to be accompanied by some kind of physical action. "I'm leaving, butthead" strongly suggests that the character will be heading for the door even as the line is said. But how many of you would be still standing in place even after you said the line? This is not unusual in a beginning actor, especially if your character has more lines to say. But if you're not moving on the line or right after it, you're probably not in the moment. In life we seldom if ever announce we are going and then make no effort to go. But this happens all the time in acting class. If you were still just standing there, you were probably thinking about the fact that you have more lines to deliver and that you'd better stay in order to say those lines. But in reality, the playwright has set up the dialogue so that the other actor will stop you if you attempt to leave, and that is just what the other actor must do. If you try to leave, the staying becomes the other actor's problem. This will be far more interesting and believable and will produce further physical action that is both believable and compelling.

"Give me the candy right now" suggests that you want the candy really badly. Your line would most certainly be accompanied by a gesture, by some movement toward the candy holder, or even by an attempt to grab it away. The grab away would certainly be a high-staked choice, both interesting and believable. Your job as an actor is to tell the story through what you do as well as what you say. Remember, the bigger the conflict, the more interesting the story. In addition, physical action conjures emotion. Physically fighting for the candy ensures that your emotional connection will not have to be generated from a mental or emotional fiction. Where your body goes, your emotions are sure to follow.

"I'll do anything you ask. Anything. Please." Sounds like begging, doesn't it? What do you do when you beg? Do you think that would be interesting to watch? Interesting to do? High-staked and powerful? Why would a good actor want to avoid such an opportunity? Did you accompany the line with an appropriate physical response?

"Oh, God, I love you, baby!" Saying this believably without appropriate physical action has to be twice as hard as committing to a physical action. People don't say things like this in a controlled and or calculated way. It is the kind of statement that explodes out of us because our emotional levels are so high. Our bodies, emotions, and thoughts are linked, interacting to make moments in which the attempt to communicate overwhelming feeling, simply put, takes charge of our entire beings. Doing less onstage simply reads as inadequate and unbelievable. It reads as "acting" in the bad sense.

Ultimately, all of our physical action and dialogue must seem spontaneous in performance, and in fact, with proper rehearsal, good actors get to the point where they can forget their homework and rehearsal and hopefully be in the moment, confident that what they have practiced for weeks will be in their bodies when called for. Athletes practice and drill, musicians practice and drill, but in performance they are in the moment. So, too, are skilled actors. It seems to me that when actors fail to make choices because they want to be spontaneous, a disservice is being done. The playwright and the audience must be served, and will that really best happen by leaving so much to the chance of spontaneous behavior? For most actors, the answer is no. That doesn't mean there is no spontaneity. We find good things to use through spontaneity in rehearsal. We keep what works as we discover things, or we add what we learn to what we already have. In other words, we build a performance—by thinking, by finding things, and by refining constantly. And, of course, we continue to find and explore things by being in the moment in performance. We change and evolve every time we step onto the stage. What we do from moment to moment, from performance to performance, should be changing in accordance to what we see and hear, just like in life. But spontaneity, for most actors, comes with the process, not instead of it. We'll discuss this process in greater detail in the next chapter.

Before we leave the subject of physical action, however, why not take one more look at the paragraph describing H.D. atop the wall? Here it is again for convenience.

Humpty sits atop the wall, exhausted from his climb. As he looks down at the hard ground below, trying to catch his breath, he becomes dizzy. His nausea weakens his resolve. He has thoughts about his happier moments in life. He becomes less sure he wants to jump. Yet he knows he must. He has never carried out anything in his life to fruition. He feels he must do this. It is essential to his broken eggo. Back and forth his thoughts go, his internal conflict, an obstacle to carrying out his objective—to end his miserable life. In the meantime, the king's men yell from below, ordering him to stay seated and to wait for them to get to him. They shout up reasons for Humpty not to kill himself. The king's men cajole, flatter, threaten, and warn him. Finally, Humpty jolts himself out of his internal conflict and tries to stand. The wind pushing against him makes this difficult to do but, faced with his own expectations and the approaching army trying to save him from himself, he overcomes self-doubt, nausea, fear of heights, and even death. Humpty pushes himself to his feet as the king's men continue to shout to him from below and look for ways to get up the wall.

Try converting each of the suggested actions to actual physical actions. Specifically write down each of the things you would do to fulfill and actualize the description. Don't write down what you will think or feel, just what you will physically do. Once you have completed writing down all your actions in chronological sequence, you will have what is called a *physical action score* (PAS). And like the score to a piece of music, your PAS will contain all the notes you will need to play physically. Try rehearsing your physical action score until you can execute all the actions from memory. Once you can, try connecting each action to the thoughts and feelings appropriate to the scene moment by moment. You may surprise yourself (and those who watch you) with how clear and compelling your work has become. You may even want to operate in the future by thinking far more in terms of what you do—that is, what you do physically as well as psychologically.

In the next chapter we'll take a closer look at how to find the story in the script and mine it for its storytelling gold.

CHAPTER THREE

ANALYSIS
TO ACTION

MANY YEARS AGO, JUST SHORTLY AFTER I HAD DECIDED
that I wanted to write about teaching the acting process effectively to high
school students, I heard Harrison Ford being interviewed on *The Actors'
Studio.* It was one of the early shows in the series, and it may have been the
first one I had actually seen. I could have thrown my arms around him when
I heard Ford say something to the effect that it was, first and foremost, "an
actor's job to tell the story." At that time I was considering working on the
book that would later become *The Actor as Storyteller,* so it did my heart good
to hear the acting icon of the day talk about seeing his job in just that light.
Since that time, I am happy to report, countless others on that same show
have, in variations of the same phrase, said the very same thing.

It is ironic, then, to have to acknowledge that most of the beginning
students I face today would never dream of what they do as actors in terms
of storytelling. Worse, most of them, if asked, wouldn't know what the story
is. Or for that matter what *a* story is. If you don't even know what a story is,
how can you possibly tell one effectively? Obviously, you can't.

In recent years, I have discovered over and over again that as a teacher I am
a victim of assumption. In the past I have assumed that my actors can read
effectively. I have assumed they could do basic analysis on a piece of material.
I have assumed they are able to look at a situation from a point of view not
necessarily their own. I have assumed they are able to listen effectively to one

another onstage. Over time, I have learned that none of these assumptions is necessarily the case and that starting at what I think is the beginning is often not the beginning enough.

Here's what I mean. I know that kids today recognize a story when they hear or see one. You are exposed to an infinite number of hours of them on television, film, and video. But you haven't necessarily learned the difference between a good story and a bad one, nor have you necessarily learned anything about how stories are painstakingly constructed, particularly good ones. More importantly, you have not necessarily learned the relation between what the writer writes and your obligation in making what's written come to life effectively and compellingly. I remember, as a kid in school, being insulted when a teacher would ask a question in an exam regarding "plot." Plot questions were too obvious, I thought then. The only thing those kinds of questions demonstrated was whether you read the book or not. They showed nothing about the higher levels of thinking that I wanted to be showing off to my literature teachers.

I bet you're not so different than the former me. You, too, probably want to show off your higher levels of acting genius. You want to concern yourself with your character's depth and variety of feeling, your character's multileveled and complex thought patterns, your character's essence. The problem is that you may not have the skills or talent to do this effectively, but more to the point, when you put your efforts into that kind of approach, you do so at the expense of your first responsibility—to tell the story of the play. The truth is that the good playwright provides plenty of complexity of character in the writing, and when you can find the simple line of action to play, the audience will find the complexity of character through what they infer by watching all the characters speak, move, and interact during the course of the play. Needless to say, the great actors find dimension in their characters that an audience might not find on its own, but if the basic storytelling is not accomplished by the actor first, then all the complexity in the world is being wasted, because the story won't get effectively communicated.

The *American Heritage Dictionary* defines *story* in its first listed definition as "an account or recital of an event or a series of events, either true or fictitious." That was the first definition I saw. I was trying to find a definition that would suit my purposes, and there it was at *numero uno*. The definition talks about events—loosely defined, things that happen. *What happens* and *what happens next* are most important to making stories, and to making them clear and compelling as actors. Aristotle told us that long ago when he said that action is the most important element of drama. Yes, characters feel and say important things, but more than anything else it is *what characters do* that makes for a good story.

So basically, what all this adds up to is the fact that a good story is composed of a series of events in a sequence, a ladder of *this happens, then this happens, then this happens*—a cause-and-effect line of action that goes from beginning to end. By recognizing this sequence of actions and seeing them as tangible items, you can begin to shape the sequence of events into moments that, in turn, can be made tangible for an audience. Without this kind of understanding, you may gloss over these storytelling moments altogether. Even if you recognize the principle of conflict and its relation to objective playing, you must also be able to recognize the arc of the story you are commissioned to tell, and shape it by connecting all the numbered cause-and-effect dots in the proper numbered sequence. You have to be able to do this if you are going to make the picture of the story clear.

If you have any doubts about whether you think in those terms when you look at a script, try doing the following exercise. It may just point out to you how unskilled you are about the basic elements of storytelling.

Read a short play or story, and then write a summary that includes only the necessary details. In other words, tell the story in your own words succinctly and clearly. Once you are finished, read it aloud—to someone else if possible; if not, just read it aloud and listen as you read. What you are likely to hear is a jumble of disorganized events, often out of order or missing one or more critical elements. You are also likely to hear a lot of descriptive information that is not necessary to the forwarding of the story, and you're apt to not hear some other detail that *is* necessary for a complete set of storytelling ingredients.

What this all points up—and this is where my assumptions keep getting me into trouble—is that even though young actors recognize stories when they hear them, they've never really paid attention to the mechanics that good playwrights use to make their stories tick like Swiss watches and run like Japanese commuter trains. It is absolutely necessary for actors to be able to do this because, ultimately, it becomes their responsibility to choose actions—physically and through spoken dialogue—that will make clear and forward the story they're helping to tell. If they aren't able to grasp and articulate the important story elements already provided, then how will they be able choose the right actions that build on what the playwright has given them? So in this chapter we'll take a look at whether you have absorbed the actor's basic necessary detective work, as well as the elements of storytelling craft laid out in earlier chapters.

Start with this:

Does the précis you wrote tell the story effectively?

If so, why; if not, why not? What is missing, what should be added, removed, and so forth if the summary is to catch the forward thrust of the story effectively?

Does the summary catch the tone and meaning of the story?

Translating tone and meaning are ultimately a part of the actor's decision-making process. Actors cannot and should not, in the end, play the idea or tone of the story, but the idea of the story and its tone can and should affect what choices actors make and the manner in which they carry them out. In the end, what actors choose to communicate must serve the overall purpose of the playwright and the director, as well as the step-by-step progression of the unfolding story.

Okay, here is the next step. It's the one you may have tried in the introduction. Try to write the story you've read in terms of a cause-and-effect sequence that is numbered. Only the cause-and-effect actions or events of the story should be included. Your exercise might look something like this:

1. Cinderella's mother dies.
2. Her father finds a new wife.
3. The new wife and her daughters become jealous of Cinderella's beauty.
4. Cinderella's father dies.
5. Cinderella's stepmother is left her father's estate.
6. The stepmother forces Cinderella into servitude....

There is no absolute right-or-wrong answer here. The important thing is that you focus on what events are essential to the story—remember, that's the only way the story will unfold clearly. Events may be added or subtracted depending on the narrative and point of view, but any successful summary will have a beginning, middle, and end, with the dots of the individual events of the story each in its proper place. Again, you are likely to find the exercise more difficult and provocative than it initially sounds.

If you are interested in further developing your story analysis and sequencing skills, you can take your cause-and-effect sequence even further. This additional step will help you develop your ability to analyze dialogue and stage direction as an actor. It will help you take apart a script in terms of its *literal, contextual,* and *subtextual* meanings, as well as help you make choices that contribute to the effectiveness of the story being told. For now, suffice it to say *literal meaning* refers to the simple meaning of the words or sentences without a context. *Contextual meaning* refers to their meaning when placed in the circumstances of the story, and *subtextual meaning* refers to what the speaker really thinks or feels at the time the words are spoken (more on this later). Here's the game:

Take your cause-and-effect sequence and now turn it into a short scene with limited stage direction. That means for each event you've listed, write a scene or episode consisting of a very limited amount of dialogue exchanged between characters that delineates the event. (I suggest two or three lines for each character, maximum.) The converted sequence might look something like the following:

1. *At* CINDERELLA's *mother's deathbed.*

   MOM: Take care of your father for me.
   CINDERELLA: I will, Mother; don't worry.

2. FATHER *enters* CINDERELLA's *room.*

   DAD: I have something important to tell you, dear. I am to be married again.
   CINDERELLA: Oh, Father. What wonderful news!

3. *In the kitchen.* CINDERELLA *enters in her late mother's dress.*

   STEPMOTHER: I thought for a moment that you ... You have no need for such a dress! Get to work.
   CINDERELLA: I will ... Stepmother.

Doing this for yourself will help sensitize you to what a playwright actually does when he or she writes a script. It will force you to pare down each of the events into its dramatic essence and require you to communicate through the implication of your dialogue far more than what the line out of context might seem to say. This, of course, is exactly what writers do, and it is what you must learn to read for. As playwrights know, and actors must learn to appreciate, dialogue operates on several levels—the literal, the contextual, and the subtextual. You must learn to see dialogue not only in terms of what it actually says, but in terms of what it suggests. Anyone who has ever dealt with Chekhov knows just what I'm talking about.

It might be worth taking a moment or two to examine this sample dialogue for what it says and what it might imply given the circumstances of the unfolding situation. This is what good actors must be able to do, and it is the kind of thing that, for the most part, actors learn or fail to learn totally on their own. It is essential, however, that you learn it. Your approach might go something like this:

1. *At* CINDERELLA'*s mother's deathbed.*

   MOM: Take care of your father for me.
   CINDERELLA: I will, Mother; don't worry.

In this first scene, of course, it is the stage direction that sets up the drama in the scene—*Cinderella's mother's deathbed.* Her mother is about to die. *Deathbed* provides the context and springboard for subtext that makes the stakes and urgency of the scene so huge. It is clearly not just the lines that are important here; it is what the lines imply. The scene is all about what is not said as much as what is and what might have been. "Take care of your father for me" is fraught with irony, in that soon Cinderella will not even be able to take care of herself. There is no dialogue that speaks directly about the mother and daughter's love for each other or about the situation, though certainly the characters must be feeling this intensely. Do Cinderella and her mom love each other dearly? Is this the best choice for making the story work? If so, how can this love be portrayed? Or perhaps mom and daughter never liked each other too much. Which makes for a better story?

It will be up to you to communicate your choices for the story through how you say what you say and what you do physically. When Cinderella says,

"I will, Mother; don't worry," what is she thinking? In other words, what is her subtext? Is she trying to convince her mother that she will take care of her dad, or is she simply covering her own fear of the future, not to mention the pain of impending loss? More importantly, which choices make for the best storytelling—a courageous stiff-upper-lipped Cinderella, or a fearful child struggling to keep it together? These kinds of choices are not spelled out in the script but are part of the actor-as-storyteller's primary obligation.

2. *Father enters* CINDERELLA'*s room.*

> **DAD:** I have something important to tell you, dear. I am to be married again.
> **CINDERELLA:** Oh, Father. What wonderful news!

Note that Dad says he has something *important* to say. That is his choice of words. He doesn't say something *fabulous* or *wonderful*—the adjective is simply "important." Is this intentional? Does he realize that Cinderella will not be happy with this news, or is the playwright just saving the *wonderful* for the exclamation of surprise that follows in the next line? What exactly is the subtext here? Will the story be better if Dad is a blind fool, or have his wife-to-be and her daughters duped him to get his money? What do later elements of the story provide as clues? What will make for the best storytelling choices? Again, all part of the actor's responsibility. Perhaps, in part, the answers have been provided in the casting. Does Dad naturally come off as sweet and stupid, or as a sensitive, kind avoider of conflict? Which is, or would be, the better choice? Why? All this is part of the storytelling obligation that must be defined and executed.

Cinderella's dialogue response, "Oh, Father" could easily be interpreted as a good thing at face value—its *literal* level. But *oh* can suggest many things, including shock and pain. What is Cinderella feeling at this moment? What choice is best for the story as it unfolds? Being initially happy might give the overall story a bigger arc. It might allow Cinderella to go through a number of discoveries before realizing she's in big trouble later in the story. But it might make her look slow, as well. The way this particular script is organized scene by scene will help suggest how it is best to play it to make the story work. The important lesson here is you need to think in these terms. Cinderella then says, "What wonderful news." On the literal level, the lines suggest joy, but on *contextual* and *subtextual* levels, is that what Cinderella really means? Is it better for the storytelling that her father believes her, or not? Should Dad register her lack of commitment, or should he be blind to it, et cetera et cetera? Without thinking in terms of the story potential and mechanics, all of these questions will find only random answers, not exactly the best bricks and mortar for good storytelling.

3. *In the kitchen.* CINDERELLA *enters in her late mother's dress.*

> STEPMOTHER: I thought for a moment that you … You have no need for such a dress! Get to work.
> CINDERELLA: I will … Stepmother.

In this scene, we are again faced with the issue of what stage direction implies. Cinderella enters in her late mother's dress. Why? How does she look in it? What does her stepmother think about the dress, about how Cinderella looks in that dress? About Cinderella's reasons for wearing that dress? About wearing the dress at this particular moment? We don't know the answers to any of these questions. The answers are not directly provided in the script. So instead, you will have to rely on storytelling choices—choices that will have to be made and agreed upon by the actors so that they can tell the story of the scene most effectively. Effective storytelling here must include making this scene as powerful as possible, but also making this scene fit well into the overall storytelling arc.

The script has provided some clues, however. First of all, there are the clues to be found by putting this scene in the context of the overall story arc. Then there are the lines in this scene themselves. Stepmother says, "I thought for a moment that you…" Though the line is not completed, it has implication. The first thing to be determined is what the rest of the unfinished line might have been. This, of course, will be the choice of the actor playing the stepmother, but it is a choice she will have to make by asking herself what will make for the best story. Once she has made that choice, she will have to figure out why she stops herself. Then she will have to communicate how to say all that clearly. Then Cinderella will have to make a choice, depending on what she sees and hears, about how to respond to it. In the end (only a moment of stage time, but like a little completed story in and of itself) she submits to her stepmother's will, but what has she learned about her stepmother, about herself, about the situation? How can, should, and does this information forward the story most compellingly?

There is another ellipsis after "I will." Why? What does the script intend? Then Cinderella actually refers to her stepmother as *Stepmother*. It is the first time we have heard Cinderella refer to her formally. Why does she use the term *Stepmother*? Is it her normal formal address for her stepmother, or is it meant somehow derisively? What exactly does it mean to her? How would she say it, et cetera? When you consider how much mileage we have gotten from these snippets of dialogue, imagine how much can be found in an actual script written by a first-class playwright. That is a terribly important concept that you must come to terms with. No doubt this kind of close work is a bit daunting to you, but hopefully, it is also inspirational. In some ways, actors have to be detectives, always in search of clues, but if you do it well, you will become a detective who can turn your detective work into artistry. Not such a bad goal!

Once you have finished your analysis, you might try to find some other actors to read the scene with. It might be fun to try to fill in with your acting some of the storytelling detail not fully provided by the script itself. Just keep in mind that you will be responsible for making choices that best serve the story. Ultimately, through your sequence of trial and error you will discover that when the dialogue of each segment captures its dramatic essence literally or by implication, and the sequence of scenes progresses clearly, your good acting can make the story come through. You will also learn that it is often your responsibility to fill in the gaps through your chosen actions—physically and psychologically (your objectives and tactics).

As this sequence of exercises clearly shows, there are so many choices that you must make as an actor—choices that can spell the difference in making a story work or fail. When most of us go to the theatre or to see a film, we don't consider the choices involved in making a moment or in making the overall story work—unless what we are seeing is *not* working. When a play or film is working effectively, we are in each moment, involved and committed, not judging or analyzing. We bring our analysis skills to bear only when something is not working. It is then we are thrown outside of the moment and the magic is compromised or lost. This is how it works for those of us who have an innate understanding of story or have been trained in this storytelling process.

Unfortunately, you may not yet have these skills. You are likely to have been brought up on computer games and car-crash movies that rely on spectacle and violence rather than on sequential storytelling craft and the subtleties of character building through selected actions. You may watch and like movies and television shows that seem to work simply because of their spectacle value. For many young actors today, noise is synonymous with good. Since that is too often the case, you now have the responsibility to change that. Don't assume that you have the necessary basic storytelling aesthetics, understanding, or skill. It will take a lot of work to develop them, but it is work that will pay off very quickly.

CHAPTER

SCRIPT ANALYSIS

THIS CHAPTER WILL FOCUS ON ANALYZING A SCENE, BUT
before you can successfully do that, you must first understand the mechanics
of the overall play. What follows is a series of questions you can dependably
use to develop your ability to examine a play, analyze it, and make interpretive
choices that will both help make the play work and make you look good as
an actor.

- What are the main conflicts found in the play?
- What is the central idea of the play (also called its spine)?
- What is the relationship of characters and their conflicts to the spine
  of the play?
- What is the genre of the play, and how does that affect the storytelling?
- What is the style of the play, and how will that affect the storytelling?
- What are the given circumstances of the play, and how do they affect
  the action and meaning of the play?

Structure and Plot

- What is the story of the play as witnessed by the audience
  (the basic outline of what happens)?
- What is the plot of the play (the sequence of events in detail,
  event by event)?

- What are the most dramatic moments in the play, and why they are so?
- What is the story from each character's point of view?
- What is the plot from each character's point of view?
- What is the superobjective of each character in the play?
- What do you know about each character?
- How does each character contribute to the central idea of the play?

The following section will offer further explanation on how all these questions provide the practical tools for unlocking a script. Please note that when examples were necessary to make or amplify a point, I have referred to *Romeo and Juliet,* since it is probably familiar to most of you.

OVERVIEW

WHAT ARE THE MAIN CONFLICTS FOUND IN THE PLAY?

All plays have a story of some kind, and any story requires some kind of conflict if it is going to hold an audience's attention. A playwright knows this and invariably uses conflict as the engine of a story. An actor must know this, too. You must be able to identify any and all conflicts when and where they appear, and know how to use them to build the story. Further, that story starts somewhere, and by the time it is over, there has been a journey that has led to a very different place; this journey may be a literal one, but it can also be an intellectual, emotional, or ethical one. It could also a combination of any or all of the journeys mentioned above. Along the way, some kind of conflict has developed either between characters or internally for one or more characters. There might also be obstacles in the path of this journey that provide conflict along the way. The conflicts in any play will be established, recognized, faced, and either partially or completely resolved by the play's characters. This sequence of action provides the basis for the plot of the play's story.

WHAT IS THE CENTRAL IDEA OF THE PLAY (ALSO CALLED ITS SPINE)?

Like all good works of art, a fine script contains no more or less than it should. The playwright has combined the elements of drama—plot, character, dialogue, spectacle, and music—in proportions that help support the sixth element of drama, a play's central idea. This spine holds all the other elements together. The central idea or ideas can also help actors discover the most important things to focus on and play. In *Romeo and Juliet,* the power of love is beautifully interwoven into the plot, characters, and dialogue. When you are cognizant of the play's spine, you will be better able to make choices that will work both to tell the story and to amplify its central ideas.

WHAT IS THE RELATIONSHIP OF THE CHARACTERS AND THEIR CONFLICTS TO THE SPINE OF THE PLAY?

Individual love versus interfamily hatred, the Capulets versus the Montagues, the power of romantic love versus loyalty to family, a father's will against a daughter's, Paris versus Romeo, Tybalt versus Mercutio—on and on, each of the conflicts in *Romeo and Juliet* help bring out the play's spine. Continuously throughout the play, Shakespeare builds a case for love and its potential to positively impact the world in which we live. Together, these thematic elements provide the glue that as actors you can convert into solid acting choices.

WHAT IS THE GENRE OF THE PLAY, AND HOW DOES THAT AFFECT THE STORYTELLING?

Shakespeare calls his play a tragedy, and even if *Romeo and Juliet* does not meet the classical definition of the genre, clearly, being labeled a tragedy tells us that the ending, if the play is to work, should make us feel sad, really sad. How can the actors ensure that this will happen? That is the question you should be asking once you recognize the genre of the play. Recognizing whether a play is a comedy, melodrama, farce, and so on will help you see a play in a particular context, which in turn should lead to a body of specific choices. In *Romeo and Juliet,* for instance, knowing we should feel sad at the end suggests that we should like the main characters, and that if the end is very sad, the beginning should be joyful, because that gives the actors in the story a more interesting journey to make. Often, young actors choose to play "doomed" at the beginning because they have read the end. Clearly, playing that choice will make the audience less likely to root for our protagonists if we are led, early on, to see the love affair as a bad idea.

WHAT IS THE STYLE OF THE PLAY, AND HOW WILL THAT AFFECT THE STORYTELLING?

The term *style* is a companion to the term *genre*. Whereas the genre is the type of play, the style is the manner in which the play is presented. Is the play an example of realism, absurdism, naturalism, theatricalism, and so on, or some combination? A more useful way of talking about style might be to refer to "the world of the play." Realism, for instance, will not work with Shakespeare. The language precludes it. Though we want our audience to believe what they are seeing and hearing, the poetry of Shakespeare requires a style that realism simply won't support. Identifying the world in which the play exists becomes an important component to making choices that will work, for all of the actors must inhabit the same fictional world if the audience is to believe in it, but the world created must be consistent with the material being presented.

WHAT ARE THE GIVEN CIRCUMSTANCES OF THE PLAY, AND HOW DO THEY AFFECT THE ACTION AND MEANING OF THE PLAY?

The characters in a play carry the values, beliefs, customs, and mores of their own time and place, and those may be far different than those of our own. The success of the story being presented hinges on the audience's ability to understand and view the play with the same eyes and ears as the characters. Otherwise, the play will not make sense. It is up to you to make choices that make clear the given circumstances necessary to make the audience believe. Life in Renaissance Verona is far different than life in late twentieth-century Lincoln, Nebraska. What differences need to be emphasized and clarified to make *Romeo and Juliet* work?

STRUCTURE AND PLOT

WHAT IS THE STORY OF THE PLAY AS WITNESSED BY THE AUDIENCE (THE BASIC OUTLINE OF WHAT HAPPENS)?

The key words here are "as witnessed by the audience." Too often actors, especially young ones, will examine a play from the point of view of a particular character rather than sitting back as an audience would to take in the whole picture. This is particularly true when reading for class work or for an upcoming audition. Actors are always tempted to immediately jump to an examination of the character they want to or are likely to play. But doing so is really like trying to determine where some of the puzzle parts fit, without knowing what the finished jigsaw puzzle actually looks like. Imagine the play *Hamlet* understood only from the point of view of Horatio or Ophelia. Imagine how diminished the love story between Romeo and Juliet would be without seeing how their love fits into the framework of the larger story.

WHAT IS THE PLOT OF THE PLAY (THE SEQUENCE OF EVENTS IN DETAIL, EVENT BY EVENT)?

Once you have determined what the overall story of the play is, you are ready to examine the plot event by event. You will learn how from the "inciting incident"—the event that triggers everything that happens after—one event brings about the next and the next, until the plot has been finally resolved. You will come to recognize how the elements of plot—the exposition and rising action, the climax, the falling action and resolution—work together to provide structure and clarity to the unfolding story. You will also learn how these events are individually arranged in sequence by the playwright to ensure that the story moves along in a compelling way for the audience. With an examination of *Romeo and Juliet,* you will come to recognize that Shakespeare formalizes his plots by dividing his play into five acts, each reflecting the plot development up to that point. When you realize this, it will be easier for you to isolate the most dramatic events in each act because you are now ready to examine smaller pieces of the overall puzzle.

WHAT ARE THE MOST DRAMATIC MOMENTS IN THE PLAY, AND WHY?

After the events of the play have been pinpointed and defined, you will want to isolate the big moments they contain. If the definition of good acting includes "telling the best possible story while serving the script," then clearly these moments will provide you with the playing area for doing so. Since the artistic rule of thumb "less is more" is in effect when acting, good actors will take every opportunity to make big and clear choices in the moments of the play where they should be doing so. Sometimes young actors, and for that matter, even more experienced ones, choose to play every moment in the play as though it is "the" singular event of the plot. Of course, making everything important diminishes the importance of the big moments when they come. By learning to recognize the ones vital for the story during the script analysis process, your preparation work carves the path for clearer and more exciting choices later, while minimizing the chances for overacting.

WHAT IS THE STORY FROM EACH CHARACTER'S POINT OF VIEW? WHAT IS THE PLOT FROM EACH CHARACTER'S POINT OF VIEW?

Once the story and plot of a play are understood from the audience point of view, you are finally ready to examine the play from the individual points of view of the characters. For each of those characters, the story and plot are different and unique. The characters in a play don't necessarily receive all the information that the audience does. Their individual views are more subjective and dependent on who they are and what they know about the unfolding plot. It is the actors' responsibility to play their actions with only that limited information in mind. But it is critically important that all actors know how the overall play works in order to ensure that their individual contributions serve that story as a whole. The actor playing Paris, for instance, must know and understand the overall story so he can find choices that will keep his character well contrasted to that of Romeo, his rival suitor. Imagine, on the other hand, what it would do to the story if the actor playing Paris acted his role knowing Juliet had another lover on the side.

WHAT IS THE SUPEROBJECTIVE OF EACH CHARACTER IN THE PLAY?

Every character in a play must fulfill her part in creating a fully realized telling of the story. It follows, then, that each character contributes to the overall conflict or conflicts that make up the heart of the story. If that is so, then that conflict must somehow emerge from a need that that character is pursuing. The need that the character struggles to satisfy during the course of the play is the *superobjective*. Obstacles confront the character as they attempt to fulfill their objectives during the course of the play. These obstacles either take the form of other characters in pursuit of their own objectives or of circumstantial obstacles that the script provides. It is your job as an actor to find in the script the goal your individual character is pursuing; for once you do, you can begin to develop through the script a strategy that will lead you to your *throughline of action* or *arc*. You must come to realize that characters in a play, unlike people in real life, must engage in single, clear actions that come from their need to fulfill their superobjective. This might sound simplistic, but magically, when the actors do this, the script itself will fill out the complexity of each character.

The actors playing Romeo and Juliet, for instance, might determine that their superobjective is to find happiness together in marriage. All their chosen actions are an attempt to arrive at that goal. By pursuing this goal feverishly, their story becomes passionate, exciting, and clear. Lord Capulet's superobjective is to see his daughter successfully married. For him that means Paris, not Romeo. His actions are all consistent with his desire to obtain his goal, and by committing to them fully, the actor playing Capulet sets up a huge obstacle for Juliet, and later, for Romeo, to overcome. And so on and so on. Having a clear superobjective that can be played fully can lead only to clear choices and actions onstage—actions that are exciting and compelling to watch.

WHAT DO YOU KNOW ABOUT EACH CHARACTER?

In a literature class we are trained to analyze and discuss the characters in a book or play as though they are real human beings. We speculate about their motivations, their childhoods, their interior lives, and what they will do after the point at which the novel ends. But, in fact, characters from a book or play do not exist outside the pages from which they come. They exist to serve the book or play from which they spring. Creating biographies of the characters they will play can be helpful to actors, but only if those biographies help them to fulfill the responsibility of the storytelling in the play itself. The character analysis that best serves actors as they attempt to make choices that serve both the play and themselves comes from what the characters do, from what they say, from what is said about them, and from what we are told by the playwright. This is the information that can be trusted. It does not come from speculation. It comes solely from what the playwright meant for us to know. It will therefore help you do your job as storyteller and servant of the script.

HOW DOES EACH CHARACTER CONTRIBUTE TO CENTRAL IDEA OF THE PLAY?

Once all of the questions about character have been answered, it is worthwhile to examine how each character serves to reveal the spine of the play. If you can determine those answers, it will likely help you make and refine choices that will reinforce that central idea. The supporting characters in *Romeo and Juliet* are all in the play for a reason. Yes, as stated earlier, they help to tell the story of the play, but each of them also serves in some capacity to reveal the author's overall points. Benvolio, Mercutio, Tybalt, Nurse, and Friar Lawrence each contribute to the central idea of the play through their words and actions, and through their attitudes regarding the subject of love. Understanding the Nurse's appreciation for young love can help the actor playing her achieve nuances and colors she might not otherwise attain. Knowing how badly Friar Lawrence want peace in his parish and perceiving his belief in the healing power of love can help the actor playing him make committed choices when dealing with the love-stricken and, later, love-unstrung Romeo.

By the time you have worked through the questions, you can't help but have a first-rate understanding of the meaning of the play, how the play works overall, and the individual parts that, when put together, make it all work. You will understand how plot, character, and the idea behind the play interconnect to make for potentially compelling drama. You are now ready to move in closer to the material—to take a more microscopic look at the actual machinery of the play. In the next chapter, we will narrow the focus onto individual scenes and how to make them work.

SCENE ANALYSIS

OVER THE LAST SEVERAL YEARS, I HAVE CONDUCTED many workshops focusing on script analysis—some for professional actors, other for secondary-school drama teachers. The professional actors, more often than not, work in film and commercials, and many of them have had little or no theatre training. The acting classes they have taken have been hit-or-miss, usually focusing on emotional truth and sense memory rather than on dramatic analysis. Drama teachers, as many of you probably know, run the gamut from former theatre professionals to music and English teachers who have been drafted into the cause. The members of both groups often enroll in my workshops because when they look at a script, they have little or no idea what to do with it. More often than not, when I ask them what they look for when they pick up a script, those that have an answer at all usually say something like, "I read the script to get clues about my character," or "to help my actors find their characters."

I suspect that what I have just described is not at all uncommon. If asked, many of you would probably come up with a similar answer. Unfortunately, too many actors, as I mentioned in the beginning of the last chapter, think in terms of the character they are playing rather than thinking in terms of the more important whole—the script and the story it contains. The untrained or improperly trained actor tends to think of himself as the center of focus rather than as a piece of the puzzle that must fit perfectly into the fabric of the entire picture. This kind of thinking can keep a play from working effectively onstage or skew a movie in a direction not intended, especially if the actor doing it is a bankable star. The truth is that before any specific choices about character should be made, actors must be able to visualize the story contained in the script from the point of view of the audience and keep in mind the ideas behind the script they are serving. You must view that script objectively, taking in the whole story event by event, not just the story from the point of view of the character you are playing.

Thinking in terms of what the audience needs to see forces you to begin thinking about your character in terms of chosen actions rather than creating persona. It is important that you understand the idea that characters do not exist outside of the script in which they are found. If a character enters on page 3 and exits on page 37 of a script, then those 34 pages are the sum total of your character's existence. That character exists because the playwright or screenwriter needed that character to be there—to serve his or her purposes, not yours. It is your obligation to learn to begin your journey to find and play your character with that in mind.

Only after you understand how the script works dramatically as a whole can you begin to focus on the development of your individual character—in service of the script. Developing a character to play on the stage or screen is an interesting amalgam, combining the following ingredients:

- The writer's vision, suggested mostly through words
- The physical, intellectual, and emotional presence of the actor cast in the role
- The choices that actor makes for that role—physically, psychologically, and emotionally
- The physical manner in which the actor carries out those choices

When you think about it, it is no wonder, then, that no two Hamlets or Ophelias are ever quite the same. To some extent, you play yourself in every role you take on, since it is only through your own intellectual, emotional, physical, and experiential makeup that you can understand and communicate the character you portray. At the expense of repeating myself, you must never forget that the successful actor's first step in the process of finding and developing a character is to understand the script. By doing so, you ensure that the first big step you take is one that heads in the right direction.

Before any specific scene can be analyzed, the overall script must be examined, since any specific scene must be seen in the context of the action of the script in its entirety. The given circumstances of any particular scene are dependent on the accumulated circumstances that preceded the individual scene. In the last chapter, we took a look at a process for an analysis of a play overall. In this chapter the focus will be on the individual scene. Since that is the case, we will skip the examination of the play overall, by using a short play that has no context outside the single scene that is reproduced here. Keep in mind, however, that a complete scene-by-scene analysis of an entire play will create for you an arc or throughline of action far more detailed and complex than a simple scene can provide.

THE ARC —
A THROUGHLINE OF ACTION

In spite of misconceptions created by actors on talk shows, character is mostly communicated through the actions actors choose to execute and the manner in which they do so. An audience does not see the biography of the character the actor has created, nor the unspoken subtext the actor may employ. Actions, which include all the things a character says as well as carries out physically, are the tangible aspects of any performance. Only through what is tangible will an audience ultimately come to know who a character is. An audience cannot read a character's mind or look into a character's heart. An audience can only make assumptions and draw conclusions from what they see and hear. Obviously, then, the actions you choose to present to an audience are extremely important. The actions you select and perform are mostly generated by doing the following:

- determining the given circumstances at any particular moment of the play
- determining the results of an actor asking "the magic if."
- determining what a character needs and what that character is willing to risk in order to get it
- playing specific objectives
- employing tactics selected in order to obtain those objectives

DISCOVERING THE ACTION

By finding and playing the actions dictated from your investigation of the items just listed, you will create an arc or throughline of action for your character. This arc will not only define your character scene by scene, it will also suggest the changes that your character undergoes in the time that elapses between each scene. This process of creating complexity through simplicity might seem to you like cheating, but as I often tell my own students, "Good acting is, at least in part, made up of illusion." Besides, working in this manner is far more reliable than trying to magically "become the character" as so many beginning actors would like to do. Once again, the qualitative judgment of good acting is better left to the audience watching, rather than to your subjective perceptions of your own work.

You must take a fresh approach to each scene in which your character appears. It is important for you to keep in mind that characters, not unlike human beings, are made up of a combination of characteristics and contradictions that, when put together, add up to complex personalities. By focusing on the particular tasks (objectives and tactics) in each scene, and solving the particular problems you face in efficient ways, you will have created a similar complexity. You will also be telling the overall story with clarity.

However, it is also important that you keep in mind that each scene in a play is a story unto itself, and that you must approach each scene analytically in the same way you approach the overall play. It is often a good idea to begin a scene-by-scene analysis of a character's throughline or arc by selecting a scene that is immediately accessible to you—in other words, one that you already seem to understand. The discoveries made in this particular scene can help you to more easily analyze the scenes that do not seem as accessible to you at first glance.

What follows are two sets of study questions that can be used to guide you. The first refers to an analysis of the play overall found in the previous chapter; the second is for the breakdown of a specific scene. When completed, the answers to these questions should lead you to an understanding of how the play works, and to the development of actions that will help you convey the story of each scene specifically. The answers you find will also help you create and define your characters.

First, a review of the questions that must be asked when examining a full-length play in preparation for a specific scene study analysis.

1. What are the play's given circumstances, and how do they affect the play's action and meaning?

2. What is/are the main conflicts in the play?

3. What is the plot of the play—the sequence of events in detail? (What actually happens from the audience's perspective?)

4. How does the conflict between the characters relate to the spine of the play?

5. What is the genre of the play, and how does that affect the way the play is acted?

6. What are the most dramatic moments of the play, and why?

Now some questions regarding a specific scene.

1. What are the given circumstances of the specific scene?

2. What actually happens in the scene? Literally, what are the story events one by one?

3. What are the conflicts in the scene?

4. What are the most dramatic moments in the scene? What leads up to these moments of drama? Be specific.

5. What is the climax of the scene? Why?

6. How does your character contribute to the conflict in the scene?

7. What does your character need in this scene from the other character/s?

8. What are the actions your character actually performs in the scene?

9. What stands in the way of getting what your character needs?

10. What does your character do to get around these obstacles?

11. How badly does your character need what is needed?

12. What is your character willing to do to get what is needed?

13. What discoveries does your character make during the scene?

14. How does this new information affect your character? Does it change your character's behavior, way of thinking, needs?

15. Can you specifically identify the places in the script where new information is received by your character? Do so.

16. Does this information somehow change what your character thinks and/or feels? Does this news signal a victory? A defeat? A reason for reevaluation, et cetera?

17. What internal changes does your character go through at these moments?

18. Can you map a throughline of action for your character now that you have answered the preceding questions? Do so.

The answers to both these sets of questions can help guide you to an effective scene analysis and, in turn, to a set of actable choices that work for the scene and the overall play.

The play reprinted below is from *Ten-Minute Plays: Volume 3* from Actors Theatre of Louisville, edited by Michael Bigelow Dixon and Michele Volansky and published by Samuel French, Inc.

GO LOOK

CHARACTERS
KATH, *twenties*
DANNY, *twenties*

TIME AND PLACE
The present. Two a.m.
A tent in a wilderness area.

[DARKNESS. FOREST NOISES. KATH *switches on a flashlight.*]

KATH: What was that?
DANNY: Hunh?
KATH: I heard something.
DANNY: What did it sound...
KATH: Shhh.
DANNY: OK.

KATH: It's stopped.

DANNY: Good.

KATH: Go look.

DANNY: What?

KATH: Go look outside. Around the tent.

DANNY: What for?

KATH: It might be something.

DANNY: Kath…

KATH: Please.

DANNY: I'm not dressed.

KATH: Who's going to see you?

DANNY: Whatever made the noise.

KATH: It won't care if you have clothes on.

DANNY: It? What kind of it?

KATH: I don't know.

DANNY: You mean like a bear?

KATH: No. Not necessarily.

DANNY: You want me to go look for something that's not necessarily a bear. In the middle of the night. In the middle of nowhere. In my underwear.

KATH: Take the flashlight.

DANNY: Why don't you go?

KATH: You're the man.

DANNY: Right. I forgot.

KATH: I was kidding.

DANNY: No gun, no knife. But I've got the dick. What am I going to do with that? Piss on him? Fuck him?

KATH: You are gross.

DANNY: Thank you.

KATH: I was only kidding anyway—about you being the man.

DANNY: Why don't you go?

KATH: Me?

DANNY: Yeah, stuff the flashlight in your jeans. The bear will think you're *really* dangerous.

KATH: You are disgusting. Just forget it.

[*Beat.*]

41

DANNY: There aren't any bears around here.

KATH: I'm sleeping.

DANNY: There isn't a bear within a hundred miles. Snakes, maybe.

KATH: Get off of me.

DANNY: There might be one in your sleeping bag.

KATH: Quit!

DANNY: But no bears.

[*Beat.*]

KATH: I never said it was a bear.

DANNY: So, what? Wild animals?

KATH: No.

DANNY: Murderers? Monsters? Your mother?

KATH: Shut up.

DANNY: Come on, Kath. What did you think?

KATH: What I always think in the woods.

DANNY: Which is?

KATH: That it will come for me.

DANNY: Ooooh. What?

KATH: I don't know.

DANNY: What does it look like?

KATH: I don't know.

DANNY: Now we're getting someplace.

KATH: I don't want to talk about him.

DANNY: You said "him." How do you know it's a he?

KATH: I've heard his growl. It sounds deep.

DANNY: Like this? I mean, [*Bass.*] like this?

KATH: You're a riot, Danny.

DANNY: The growling bogeyman.

KATH: It's not a bogeyman.

DANNY: If you say so.

KATH: It's a real man.

DANNY: Oh, a *real* man.

KATH: I mean a person, moron. On the outside. But inside …

DANNY: Yeah?

KATH: Rage.

DANNY: Rage?

KATH: No limits.

DANNY: Right. And where does this angry guy come from?

KATH: Far from here. Deep in the forest. Where there are no footprints, not even animal tracks. Just thick vines and roots and leaves that shine icy white in the moonlight.

DANNY: He lives there.

KATH: No. That's where he's born. Sometimes at night the leaves and vines shift, all by themselves, to make a clearing, as if an invisible hand was sweeping away the underbrush.

DANNY: Uh, oh.

KATH: The bare ground forms a mound that puckers at the top.

DANNY: Sounds like a pimple.

KATH: Danny …

DANNY: All right. Then what?

KATH: There's a groaning sound that starts way underground. It builds up, louder and louder.

He bursts out of the ground. Running. On all fours. No hesitation. Tearing over fields and rocks. Straight toward me. The closer he comes, the faster he runs. Until he sees where I am.

Then he stops on the side of a hill. He stands there. Looking down at me. At our tent, lit like a Chinese lantern. I can't see his face. But I know he's waiting. Teeth bared. Grinning. Growling.

DANNY: That's the end?

KATH: I never let myself think further than that.

DANNY: What would happen?

KATH: If he got me?

DANNY: If he got you.

KATH: I would be destroyed.

DANNY: You mean killed.

KATH: More than that. Everything. Gone.

DANNY: Why is he after you?

KATH: I attract him.

DANNY: In what way?

KATH: I don't know.

DANNY: Maybe he knows you won't face him.

KATH: What?

DANNY: You'll consent to be destroyed.

KATH: That's awful.

DANNY: But true.

KATH: No. I don't think so. You never know until the moment.

DANNY: Some people do.

KATH: They say they do.

DANNY: But not you. The innocent victim. The noble victim.

KATH: That's a terrible thing to say.

DANNY: A worse one to be.

KATH: Why are you being so nasty?

DANNY: Because I hate this shit. An angry Man erupts out of the night. He's going to destroy the Woman. It's straight out of a cheap horror movie. I can't stand all this self-righteous...

KATH: Danny...

DANNY: Poor, helpless you. Big, bad men. I'm sick of taking the blame.

KATH: Shut up a second. I heard it again.

[THEY *listen. Silence.*]

KATH: Turn off the flashlight. [HE *does so.*]

DANNY: That won't matter.

KATH: Why not?

DANNY: He doesn't have eyes.

KATH: How do you know?

DANNY: You said so.

KATH: No. I didn't.

DANNY: Well, he doesn't. He doesn't need them. He knows where he's going. From the instant he comes out of the ground. Spit out of the earth like something rancid.

KATH: Are you making fun of...

DANNY: Running. Speeding over hills, tree stumps, a dry creek bed. Sharp stones cut his feet. Racing, fast as a pulse. Closer. On the horizon. Closer. On the hillside. He pauses.

KATH: All right, Danny.

DANNY: Facing but not seeing. No eyes. Or nose. A blank face. A jagged hole of a mouth. Breathing fast. Grinning. Now he's ready. He starts moving.

KATH: Stop. I mean it.

DANNY: Sweeping down the hill. Toward the dark tent. Doesn't need eyes or nose. Not stalking. Drawn. Reeled in. Fast. Almost here. Outside the tent. Growling.

KATH: Quit!

DANNY: Through the flap. Past you. And into me. [HE *turns on the flashlight.*]

KATH: OK. The end. Roll the credits.

DANNY: I know your Wild Man, Kath. I've met him.

KATH: The movie's over.

DANNY: Whenever we go to the woods. And other times. The line gets stretched very thin. I could cross it. Couldn't you?

KATH: I don't know what you mean.

DANNY: I mean I know I could do terrible things. Violent things.

KATH: You're serious.

DANNY: For me, it would be easy. I could pick up a hammer or a flashlight and pound everyone and everything into pulp. Even the people I love most in the world. Pick it up and do it. And sometimes I want to, I really want to, for no reason at all. It pulls at me. Don't you ever feel that way?

KATH: I don't know.

DANNY: If you did, you'd know it

KATH: Everybody has bad thoughts, Danny.

DANNY: It's not the thoughts. That's not it. It's what's underneath. The exhilaration. The savage, howling joy of hurting. Or killing. The release. That's what makes me wonder what I am.

[*Beat.*]

KATH: I don't know what to say.

DANNY: Well, you're a fucking saint.

KATH: No. It scares me.

DANNY: It must be the testosterone talking. Since I'm the man.

KATH: I'm going to sleep.

[*Pause.*]

KATH: Danny?

DANNY: What?

KATH: Last weekend at Mother's. It was a nice day. She told me to push her out on the back patio.

DANNY: So?

KATH: She said something. I don't remember what. Not very nasty, not for her. Something about my shoes. It was nothing, really. But for an instant I felt like letting go. Just letting go and watching gravity work. I imagined her chair rolling down the slope, over the edge, and bouncing down the back steps. All the way to the garage. And when the police and ambulance would come, I'd be crying and sobbing and explaining. But inside I'd be dancing.

DANNY: But you didn't do it.

KATH: No.

DANNY: Too bad. We haven't been dancing for a long time.

[*Beat.*]

KATH: When you have those thoughts—do you have them toward me, too?

DANNY: Yes. Sometimes. I'm sorry, Kath.

KATH: But you don't do anything.

DANNY: No. Not so far.

KATH: So far, so good.

[*Beat. There is a* DISTINCT SOUND *in the woods.*]

KATH: What's that?

DANNY: I don't know. [HE *moves to exit.*]

KATH: Wait. [SHE *rises.*] Let's go.

[THEY *exit together. Curtain.*]

THE END

A good ten-minute play operates like a full-length play, in that it is often far more complicated than its simple action might suggest at first glance. Since good theatre should be enlightening as well as entertaining, the good play often carries some sophisticated ideas about the human condition intertwined with its action, character, and dialogue. I believe that *Go Look* is such a play. Though its characters exist only on the pages contained here, they clearly have a past (implied through the dialogue), and the actions they display in this scene are greatly influenced by that fact. The simple action of the play becomes far more complex when seen through the backstory suggested. *Go Look* was chosen for just this reason. It operates much like a full-length play. So before we begin an examination of the work as a practical model for scene analysis, let's take a look at it first in overview—as though it were a longer play.

All but two questions from the overview questions above appear on the list of scene study questions, as well. When analyzing a full-length play, those questions would need to be answered in both contexts. Since questions regarding the overall play should be addressed first as part of the overview of the play, let's begin our examination there, keeping in mind that in a multi-scene play the questions asked might be the same, but the answers would not. Please note that the responses to the questions below are not necessarily complete. They are offered only as a guide to how you might proceed in your analysis with the plays you might work with in the future.

GIVEN CIRCUMSTANCES OF THE PLAY AND HOW THEY AFFECT THE PLAY'S ACTION AND MEANING

You must always be specific about the details of the given circumstances in any play or scene in order to play it well. Although you should refrain from playing emotions directly, you must, as part of the given circumstances, recognize the emotional context at the starting point of any scene to be played and let it be present in the work, though not the focal point of attention. The importance of the given emotional circumstances will become clearer in a moment.

In the play *Go Look*, the who, what, when, and where go something like this. Kath and Danny are a couple in their twenties who have been together for some time. The length of their relationship is not specifically stated, though through implication, it is long enough for them to think they know each other well. They are camping alone. It is two a.m., and they are huddled their tent. It is not clear whether Kath has been awakened by a noise or has heard a noise as the couple are about to go to sleep. Two a.m. probably suggests the former, which ups the stakes at the top of the play. It is clear from the opening dialogue that whatever Kath heard has indeed upset her. Danny's first dialogue is "Hunh?," suggesting that he was asleep, almost asleep, or did not hear the noise.

If the specifics are not stated or implied in the dialogue, as actors you are free to make any choices you wish regarding the given circumstances. Whatever you select, however, the choices must be justified by the script, or not contradict the script in any way. Given circumstances should be chosen because they help make the story as exciting as possible. If it were up to me, I would have the characters awakened by a noise in the middle of the night. It makes the situation more extreme. A man and a woman awakened from sleep to face a frightening but unknown danger forces them to quickly focus and adjust. To add to that mix, their attitudes about being a man or a woman, and their expectations, fair or not, about how the opposite sex should behave under these circumstances, definitely make for a dramatic scenario.

WHAT IS/ARE THE MAIN CONFLICTS IN THE PLAY?

The driving conflict of the play concerns who will go into the night and risk personal safety in order to save them both from the potential danger outside. Each character's need for the other to be the braver one causes them to use a series of tactics whereby they end up discovering and confessing many things about themselves that otherwise might never have been exposed.

WHAT ACTUALLY HAPPENS IN THIS SCENE?

Once both characters hear the noise, they debate on who will leave the tent to find out what the noise is. Kath believes it may be a bear and quickly comes to the conclusion that it should be Danny who goes—because he is the man, contradicting contemporary and enlightened values concerning gender equality. Danny calls her on her retreat to gender typing, mostly because he doesn't want to be the one to risk going out into the night. Kath admits that she doesn't really think it is a bear, and Danny presses her to find out what she does think it is. Though Kath can't say for certain, she uses a masculine pronoun for whatever it is. Danny jumps on this and presses further. Kath admits to imagining a terror that is more dreamlike than real, a terror lodged in primitive or childhood fear rather than a belief that a dangerous animal lurks nearby. This nightmare fantasy, which she has had before (implied in the script), always ends with the creature staring at her from a distance but proceeding no further. Danny presses Kath again—this time to get her to speculate on what would happen if the creature got her. Kath admits the creature would destroy her, and Danny suggests it is more a result of Kath's allowing it to happen, a result of her unwillingness to confront the creature. He tells her she is at fault for allowing herself to be the victim, and he resents the fact that she blames men for her helplessness. After the couple hears the noise again, Danny offers his version of the story, a version both funny and scary, and one that ends with the creature pouncing on him. After getting a good scared reaction from Kath, Danny says he knows who the wild man is. He admits to having a rage inside himself that comes out periodically—a rage that is indeed violent and scary. Kath, when asked, denies that she possesses such rage and seems truly upset that Danny has confessed to such feelings. Danny suggests that Kath sees it as another frightening "man" thing. After a silence, Kath slowly admits to possessing this kind of anger toward her mother, who is a mean and controlling woman in a wheelchair dependent on Kath in part because of her handicap. Kath asks if Danny ever has similar feelings of rage toward her (Kath). Danny admits he does—on occasion. Kath accepts the news and is interrupted by the sound again. This time Danny moves to exit the tent. Kath stops him, and after a moment, they exit together.

By relating the cause-and-effect sequence of the action of the play, you can see how the playwright has structured one event coming from each previous one. If it is difficult for you to find the cause-and-effect story without missing important steps, you can work backward from the end of the play. This approach makes it unlikely that any action points will be overlooked. The net result of this process will allow you to see the events that you must shape and clarify when you begin to put the work on its feet.

HOW DOES THE CONFLICT BETWEEN THE CHARACTERS RELATE TO THE SPINE OF THE PLAY?

The conflict of the play leads Kath and Danny into a big argument, followed by honest confessions of personal feelings that are less than pretty. The confessions of both Danny and Kath seem to suggest that each of us harbors hidden feelings, not all of them pleasant, and some, like rage, are primitive and even violent. Once Kath and Danny come clean to each other, their honesty seems to have brought them closer together and they are better able to face their fears—together, as a team. Though not stated directly, the fact that they face the monster together at the end of the play seems to carry the idea behind the action. The good play doesn't preach, and the action here leads directly to a resolution that allows the audience to draw conclusions about the point of the play without it becoming didactic.

WHAT IS THE GENRE OF THE PLAY, AND HOW DOES THAT AFFECT THE WAY THE PLAY IS ACTED?

The play is scary and suspenseful. After all, it is the middle of the night in the middle of nowhere, and the boogeyman may be lurking a few steps away. Most of us have had such an experience in our lives and can identify. The play is also funny. The characters have senses of humor, and the audience's empathy for the characters in this situation will probably provoke them to laugh. But in spite of potential laughs, the play is both serious and realistic. Therefore, the actors need to make believable choices. As a good actor, you will discover where the laughs are and make choices that allow the laughs to be there, but will not do so in a way that compromises the integrity of the realistic situation.

We'll pick up question F as question 4 in the scene study questions in a moment. Note, however, that the scene questions are asked from the point of view of the characters rather than from the audience's point of view. By the time you are doing a scene-by-scene analysis, you must be thinking in terms of the conflict generated between your character and those you are working with. Therefore, you must be thinking in terms of your own character's needs and how you can satisfy those needs through the characters with whom you are sharing the scene. In other words, you must now be thinking in terms of what actions you will be playing.

WHAT ARE THE MOST DRAMATIC MOMENTS IN THE SCENE? WHAT LEADS UP TO THESE MOMENTS OF DRAMA? BE SPECIFIC.

By picking out the most dramatic moments of the scene, you can look at the step-by-step progression between those big moments as a road map leading to the big-city destinations. You will be sure to build the journey between cities so that the big moments have the payoffs they deserve—payoffs that will make the action work with maximum dramatic effect. You might want to list in chronological order the big moneymaking moments in *Go Look,* so that you can see how having this road map will help you shape the work if you were to rehearse it later on. You will soon come to realize that by doing so, you are ensuring that the story you are telling will be a good one.

WHAT IS THE CLIMAX OF THE SCENE? WHY?

If we follow the basic rules of dramatic structure, each time the boogeyman is heard from in the play is a little climax, or certainly close to it. And each time the boogeyman comes a-calling needs to be more climactic than the previous one, since good dramatic action demands an effective dramatic progression. Besides the plot of "will the main characters be eaten?," there is also the unfolding plot of what each of the characters' metaphorical boogeyman story reveals about them as individuals. This plotline eventually leads to the confessions made by both Danny and Kath concerning the rage that lies buried within them. These confessions, in some ways, are as climactic as the more obvious plotline and really elevate the story above a simple situational play. These ugly revelatory confessions require that the characters really push each other during the course of the play, so that it is clear to the audience that these confessions are meant to have been kept secret because of their ugliness. These secrets, in turn, make the confessions big dramatic payoffs that are both earned and dramatically rewarding.

HOW DOES YOUR CHARACTER CONTRIBUTE TO THE CONFLICT IN THE SCENE?

It will be essential that you make and play out the connection between conflict and objective. The climaxes referred to in the previous question grow out of the logical conclusion to the conflicts described earlier. These conflicts will be created and sustained by the actors playing the characters pursuing their objectives—at all times. The tactics and objectives played all come from the need to win, to make the other character be the one to go outside the tent or, in the parallel plot, admit to what is really being carried around inside them. The script that the playwright has provided is like a railroad track requiring only that the actors drive that dramatic engine called conflict down the track. When you play your objectives at all time, you are keeping that engine from veering off that track.

WHAT DOES YOUR CHARACTER NEED IN THIS SCENE FROM THE OTHER CHARACTER/S?

Need is another term for "objective" or "intention," and the question has really been answered already. It is hard to separate objective from conflict, and once you are able to make the connection between the two and use it at all times, your work will invariably become more specific and exciting.

WHAT ARE THE ACTIONS YOUR CHARACTER ACTUALLY PERFORMS IN THE SCENE?

This question is really asking you to connect all the things you do physically and psychologically in the scene to the objectives you are playing. All physical actions chosen for the scene, as well as the purpose behind all dialogue spoken, are offered to you by the playwright to help you pursue and fulfill your objectives. When Kath insults Danny, she is doing so in order to achieve an objective, or she is employing a tactic to do so. When Danny climbs on top of Kath, he is doing so to achieve an objective, whether or not he does so consciously. The actor playing the character makes choices for that character and does so understanding more about the character than the character actually does about himself. Remember, as the actor playing the character, you have already read the play and know your obligations to the story of the play that must be fulfilled. In life, we don't necessarily possess an awareness about the actions we carry out—certainly not at all times. But as actors, we must make choices for our characters that add up to clarity for the audience watching. Unless these choices are thought through and selected, there is no guarantee that the audience will see what they are supposed to.

WHAT STANDS IN THE WAY OF GETTING WHAT YOUR CHARACTER NEEDS?

The acting term here is *obstacles*—the things that stand in the way of getting what is needed. Obstacles are devices that actors can identify and use to make their characters' needs more difficult to obtain and thus increase the conflict or up the stakes in any scene. Fear is a big obstacle in this scene. Since both Kath and Danny are petrified of what may be lurking outside, each wants the other to "go look." That simple fact helps provide obstacles for each of them constantly and helps generate the major conflict in the scene. In terms of the other big conflict of the scene—facing the rage each of them keeps buried inside—the difficulty in admitting the ugly truth about themselves also provides obstacle power and ups the difficulty factor to confessing.

WHAT DOES YOUR CHARACTER DO TO GET AROUND THESE OBSTACLES?

HOW BADLY DOES YOUR CHARACTER NEED WHAT IS NEEDED?

WHAT IS YOUR CHARACTER WILLING TO DO TO GET WHAT IS NEEDED?

Questions 10–12 are all closely linked, and when answered fully and specifically, those answers can really get you onto the track that will lead you to keeping the scene exciting. The answers will also help you find choices that will aid in your creation of character. The way the actor playing Kath fights physically and psychologically to get Danny to be the one to "go look" will demonstrate character. The way the actor playing Danny uses Danny's sense of humor as written in the script to combat Kath and to break her down demonstrates character. So does his willingness to confess that he has tremendous rage. The tactics you choose to fulfill your character's needs are conveyed totally through what you say and what you do during the course of the scene.

When and where do the characters touch with affection? How far does each character go physically to get the other out of the tent? When does Kath want to be held, to be kissed, to be loved physically? Her physical actions must tell us. When does Danny show affection, or use his stronger physicality to get what he needs? When does he control Kath with his physical dominance, when with his verbal power? The tactics selected by each actor invariably lead to physical or verbal actions that help tell the story with clarity and excitement, while defining character—all at the same time.

CONCLUSIONS

Once you have completed your independent analysis of the script with this kind of detail, you are ready to begin your rehearsal process, with your scene partners for class, or with the company of players beginning a production rehearsal. All of the choices you will have made, of course, are subject to change, based on the practical need to do so. If the scene is being prepared for class, your scene partners may have drawn different conclusions in their independent analyses, and you will have to accommodate each other while trying to execute a shared vision of the scene that works effectively. That is part of the process. If you are developing a role for production, the director has the final say, and all choices, by every actor, will have to ultimately blend together to produce the effective whole that the director is responsible for creating. In either case, however, the analysis work done can only help you bring an understanding of the play to the first rehearsal—an understanding that will help all concerned get on the right track and headed in the direction that the engine of the play must travel.

CHAPTER SIX

SCORING
THE SCENE

IN THE LAST CHAPTER WE WENT THROUGH THE PROCESS
of reading and analyzing a script, starting with an examination of the overall
play followed by a focused analysis of a specific scene. The intent of the
chapter was to demonstrate that in order to go through the analysis process
effectively and efficiently, it is necessary to approach the material from several
points of view: that of the audience (as represented by the director), that of
the playwright, and after those have been accomplished, that of the individual
characters inhabiting the play. As an actor, it is absolutely necessary that you
have a handle on the way a particular story works overall, as well as from the
viewpoint of the individual character you are playing. Since each individual
character was created by the playwright in order to serve the overall story, it
is necessary that you have that information clearly in hand before you begin
your work with other actors. Your ultimate goal is to be able to work with
a script independently and, hopefully, become director-proof. Remember,
ultimately, behaving believably or even compellingly onstage is not enough.
If you really possess all the tools necessary for fine acting, you must be able
to make choices that bring the script to life in the manner intended by the
playwright and be able to listen and react moment by moment.

As a convenient reference, here is the list of questions we examined in the
last chapter, the answers to which should lead to an understanding of the
overall play and to the dynamics of each individual scene.

1. What are the play's given circumstances, and how do they affect the play's action and meaning?

2. What is/are the main conflicts in the play?

3. What is the plot of the play—the sequence of events in detail? (What actually happens from the audience's perspective?)

4. How does the conflict between the characters relate to the spine of the play?

5. What is the genre of the play, and how does that affect the way the play is acted?

6. What are the most dramatic moments of the play, and why?

7. What are the given circumstances of the specific scene?

8. What actually happens in the scene? Literally, what are the story events one by one?

9. What is/are the conflicts in the scene?

10. What are the most dramatic moments in the scene? What leads up to these moments of drama? Be specific.

11. What is the climax of the scene? Why?

12. How does your character contribute to the conflict in the scene?

13. What does your character need in this scene from the other character/s?

14. What are the actions your character actually performs in the scene?

15. What stands in the way of getting what your character needs?

16. What does your character do to get around these obstacles?

17. How badly does your character need what is needed?

18. What is your character willing to do to get what is needed?

19. What discoveries does your character make during the scene?

20. How does this new information affect your character? Does it change your character's behavior, way of thinking, needs?

21. Can you specifically identify the places in the script where new information is received by your character? Do so.

22. Does this information somehow change what your character thinks and/or feels? Does this news signal a victory? A defeat? A reason for reevaluation, et cetera?

23. What internal changes does your character go through at these moments?

    Can you map a throughline of action for your character now that you have answered the previous questions? Do so.

Note that Questions 1–18 were discussed specifically in the previous chapter, but questions 19–24 were not.

SCORING THE ACTION

The latter questions, 19–24, refer to issues that come up in the moment-by-moment transactions of the play and will be addressed specifically in this chapter. The earlier questions refer to an understanding of the play and scenes that actors must deal with first if they are to understand the action of the play and of the characters carrying out that action. Moment-to-moment choices cannot be created without the kind of understanding that the answers to the earlier questions provide.

Making notations directly on a script can help you find, make, and remember choices in the moments of interaction, when you also have an obligation to listen and react to your scene partners. It is one thing to analyze a text as part of your actor's homework, and it is quite another to have to apply what was learned from that homework process while attempting to act and react spontaneously in a rehearsal situation. An efficient method of scoring a scene, or breaking a scene down into its most basic components, can go a long way toward making a bridge between the isolated homework and the active and shared part of the process. Let's see how.

One of the simplest ways for you to score your work is by literally making notes on the script itself. That way the information garnered through the analysis process is available for use at the time you will need that information—while acting moment to moment. A script , of course, does not have the room to hold long-winded answers in its margins, nor will you have time to read an essay while trying to listen intently to your fellow actors. But by establishing a system of notation or scoring, you can mark your script in such a way that, like a musical score, the basic things you need to know for the playing of each scene will be right there in front of you. As you read, individually work on, or rehearse a particular scene, your scripts, like the musical score of an instrumentalist, will be ready to guide you, note by note, measure by measure, through the entire piece. These notations will serve to remind you to carry out necessary actions that might otherwise be forgotten in the early stages of the rehearsal process while you are still juggling more responsibilities than you are able to handle moment to moment.

What follows is a model for a usable system of notation for scoring a script. This suggested model can be adapted or modified to serve your own purposes. Feel free to do so. Keep in mind that if the script you are working with does not belong to you, you should photocopy it so that you do not destroy the script for others who might use it later. You might also want to enlarge the script while you are copying it, to make it easier to read and to give you more room for your own notation. Also be sure to use a pencil for all notations so that the notes taken can be easily changed. As you continue to work on your script during the rehearsal process, you will obviously learn more about the play, the scene, and your character. You will want to adjust your notations as your understanding of the play, the scene, and your character continues to evolve as a result of collaborative input and your expanded insights on the play.

NOTATION SYSTEM

1. Write at the top of the scene your overall objective for the scene.

2. Divide the scene into beats by drawing a line across the page after each beat ends. At the top of each new beat on the left side, clearly state the new objective being sought and/or the specific tactic being used.

3. On the right side of your copy of the script, write an explanation for each transition. (It could be a discovery, a new idea, a defeat, a victory, et cetera.)

4. Also use this space to briefly describe subtext and psychological and physical actions that you will eventually use to make the story tangible to an audience.

5. Look at the other characters' lines. Circle any new information (information that your character did not previously know) including stage directions hinted at through the dialogue. Remember, hearing this new information is actable.

6. Highlight or box the major dramatic moments of the scene you are doing. Double box the climax.

NOTATION SYSTEM EXPLAINED

1. Write at the top of the scene your overall objective for the scene.

   The overall objective listed at the beginning of a scene, or for that matter, any specific beat objective or tactic, should contain a strong, specific verb, one that can be accomplished by using the other actor in the scene. In other words, it should be a goal or need that you really can obtain from the other actor or, at the least, require involvement between the two of you. Starting an objective with the phrase "to make...," as in "to make Danny feel small," connects you with the other actor or actors and can be accomplished in a tangible way. It is a goal that when accomplished can be seen in the other actor. If this serves the needs of the character in the script and supports what is happening in that section of the play, then this is a good objective, because it definitely is doable and is connected to the other actor.

   Note that not every scene has a single objective that can be played from the beginning to the end of a scene, but surprisingly many do. The trick is finding that single objective that clearly covers the scene—simply, clearly, and logically. If you have trouble identifying that single objective, or an objective that reflects the action of a particular section of a scene, you will have to step back and examine the scene from the position of the audience and review the scene's throughline or arc. This should help you isolate the conflict that generates the action and objective.

   By the time you have answered the questions listed, you will have discovered the conflict in the scene, and question 13 asks about objective specifically. Remember that objectives that can be clearly, strongly, and simply stated are likely to make for objectives that can be played in the same manner. For objectives that are not easily and clearly expressed, the opposite is too often the case. Writing the selected objective at the top of the scene quickly gives the measure of its utility. If what is written can be played throughout the scene and keeps the scene on track with a logical progression that is dramatically interesting, chances are it is an effective and well-chosen action to play.

Keep in mind that any notation system you use should not be treated in the same manner that the struggling student treats his algebra class—"If I can get down the mechanics, I can pass this course." Developing the ability to isolate a playable objective is a key to making a scene work and making your work effective. An arbitrary or fuzzy decision hastily scribbled on the script just to get it out of the way is one that you will quickly forget or ignore altogether, ensuring that the process has been a waste of time.

In cases where no single objective runs through the entire scene, there are usually big transitional moments where a particular objective is given up and replaced by another, usually as a result of a victory, defeat, discovery, or interruption. There will be more on transitional moments later. Critical to using any specific objective is the understanding and commitment by you to play your objectives at all times, unrelentingly. Though focusing on objectives at all times may seem simplistic and not necessarily in line with how people behave in real life, by using this tool you will stay on the tracks of the story. The audience will add any necessary additional complexity from what they know as they watch. In spite of the propaganda, acting is not like life; it just looks like it when well done. It is an actor's job to help tell the story of the play. To accomplish this end, you must choose from an infinite variety of actions, the ones that will best tell that story. Selecting the right objectives can help you accomplish this goal. Otherwise, the play will remain a maze containing an infinite number of pathways, most leading to dramatic dead ends.

2. Divide the scene into beats by drawing a line across the page after each beat ends. At the top of each new beat on the left side, clearly state the new objective being sought and/or the specific tactic being used.

Some acting approaches refer to all playable actions as objectives; others use the term *tactics* to refer to smaller action units in which a particular strategy is used to pursue the overall objective. Regardless of the terminology you choose to employ, each time there is a strategy change or a complete change in objective, there is a transition. A line should be drawn across the script each time that occurs. The line will give you a visual marker that tells you that you must execute a transition and move on to a new strategy or objective. Let's examine the opening of *Go Look* from the point of view of the actor playing Kath and see how this works.

OBJECTIVE:
TO MAKE DANNY DEAL WITH THE PROBLEM OUTSIDE

TACTIC: TO GET DANNY'S ATTENTION

KATH: What was that?
DANNY: Hunh?
KATH: I heard something.
DANNY: What did it sound…
KATH: Shhh.
DANNY: OK.

TACTIC: TO GIVE DANNY USEFUL INFORMATION

KATH: It's stopped.
DANNY: Good.

TACTIC: TO MAKE DANNY GO INVESTIGATE

KATH: Go look.
DANNY: What?
KATH: Go look outside. Around the tent.
DANNY: What for?
KATH: It might be something.
DANNY: Kath…
KATH: Please.

TACTIC: TO CONVINCE DANNY THAT BEING DRESSED DOES NOT MATTER

DANNY: I'm not dressed.
KATH: Who's going to see you?
DANNY: Whatever made the noise.
KATH: It won't care if you have clothes on.
DANNY: It? What kind of it?

TACTIC: TO AVOID DANNY'S CONCERN ABOUT WHAT "IT" MIGHT BE

KATH: I don't know.
DANNY: You mean like a bear?
KATH: No. Not necessarily.
DANNY: You want me to go look for something that's not necessarily a bear. In the middle of the night. In the middle of nowhere. In my underwear.
KATH: Take the flashlight.
DANNY: Why don't you go?

TACTIC: TO MAKE DANNY GO BY ATTACKING HIS MANHOOD

KATH: You're the man.
DANNY: Right. I forgot.
KATH: I was kidding.
DANNY: No gun, no knife. But I've got the dick. What am I going to do with that? Piss on him? Fuck him?
KATH: You are gross.
DANNY: Thank you.
KATH: I was only kidding anyway—about you being the man.
DANNY: Why don't you go?
KATH: Me?
DANNY: Yeah, stuff the flashlight in your jeans. The bear will think you're *really* dangerous.
KATH: You are disgusting. Just forget it.

[*Beat.*]

Note that the beat changes for Kath might not match where the beat changes are for Danny. The actors playing the roles are free to analyze and score the script any way they see fit. The actor playing Kath, for instance, might find fewer beats than I did in the preceding section of the scene, but I wanted to reflect the various ways that Danny is pressed by Kath to go outside. Danny's manhood is challenged by Kath at least twice, and Kath says various things to Danny that are intended to make him give in. The three last beats above, however, might have been written as one longer beat titled "to make Danny go investigate." I marked it as I did because I wanted to demonstrate that, for Danny at least, there are several money "moments" that come as a result of Kath's tactical onslaught to get him to go outside.

3. On the right side of your copy of the script, write an explanation for each transition. (It could be a discovery, a new idea, a defeat, a victory, et cetera.)

    A *beat* is the length of script a particular objective or tactic is pursued. Beat changes, or *transitions,* occur when objectives or tactics are given up and must be replaced by new ones. These changes come as a result of victories, defeats, discoveries, or interruptions. In the cutting just presented, had Kath prevailed and gotten Danny to go outside to investigate, it would have been a victory for Kath and a defeat for Danny. This victory/defeat would have constituted a moment between them marking the end of that particular struggle or beat, a moment that would have been dramatically interesting and therefore necessary to play. In this section, however, there are no legitimate victories or defeats, but there is no shortage of discoveries, new ideas being hatched, and tactical shifts that can be turned into playable moments. Danny, especially, must take in several attacks by Kath, as previously pointed out, and make adjustments to them. The discovery that his manhood is being attacked, for instance, requires a moment of discovery before a response can be mounted. And the discovery that the "it" outside may be an "IT" is certainly food for thought, food that dramatically cannot be ignored. For Kath, there is the finding of new tactics to persuade her partner to "take arms against a sea of troubles." Multiple attacks on Danny's manhood and suggesting the flashlight are examples of this. What exactly goes through each character's mind during these moments of the play is the subtext that you and your partner must provide for yourselves and, that, once created, must somehow be conveyed to the audience. Notation 4 can help with this. Also note that the opening beat starts with a discovery before the dialogue. Kath must hear the noise before she asks about it.

4. Also use this space to briefly describe subtext and psychological and physical actions that you will eventually use to make the story tangible to an audience.

    It is important to remember that dialogue is only one part of your storytelling obligations. What a character says is not necessarily what he means, and what a character is thinking and feeling might not be reflected by what that character says. Playwrights provides only the skeleton of the story in their written dialogue and fully expect the actor to fill in the rest. Part of this unprovided story will be discovered through the rehearsal process, but as an actor you must develop the habit of filling in gaps as you do your preparation homework. By penciling in this kind of psychological subtext on your script once you have thought through how one moment leads to another, you will have it available for use while you rehearse. Of course, as you learn more during the rehearsal process, your penciled-in commentary can be changed as your developing interpretation becomes clearer.

    You can also begin thinking about the ways you can use physical action to get what you need in the scene. A playwright may provide some stage direction and some clues to what is happening physically through the dialogue, but much of what occurs physically in the story comes as a result of what you and your director come up with. In a production situation, the director may provide you with much of the physical story or may work collaboratively with the actors to do so; but in a scene study situation, it is up to you to provide your own blocking choices entirely. That means you will need to think about what works and what doesn't on your own. Whether you come up with a good choice spontaneously while rehearsing or as a result of some good homework thinking, you will want to notate these choices in your script so that they are not forgotten. Again, they can be changed as necessary when more is learned, or when a better choice is developed.

5. Look at the other characters' lines. Circle any new information (information that your character did not previously know), including stage directions hinted at through the dialogue. Remember, hearing this new information is actable.

Actors have a tendency to not listen onstage, and listening is often the key to the best kind of acting—the kind that seems totally spontaneous and of the moment. The most common reasons for failing to listen well onstage include concentrating on remembering your lines, thinking about what you are going to do next, and focusing on your own actions rather than those of the other actors in the scene. All of these activities should be taken care of as part of the homework process, or as part of the necessary early struggles in rehearsal. However, there comes a time when you must be totally available to see and hear what is going on in the actual moment-by-moment work onstage. This is what people do in real life, and it is certainly the one thing that actors must do, as well—if they are going to successfully create the illusion of reality. It is also the activity most likely to produce surprisingly original and compelling choices. By identifying as part of the homework process the important information that the other characters throw your way, you can be better prepared to listen for these lines and respond to them. By marking those pieces of dialogue in your script, you give yourself a useful visual reminder to do so.

6. Highlight or box the major dramatic moments of the scene. Double box the climax.

It is important to keep in mind that playwrights write scenes centered on a conflict that builds toward some kind of climax and resolution. Too often, actors don't think in these terms. Instead they choose to wander through the scene, hoping to stumble upon the key that opens its doors, preferring to leave thoughts about structure to playwrights and directors. But in fact, when actors make choices that recognize and build on the provided dramatic structure, they are more apt to make choices that usefully exploit what the playwright has given them. By boxing the dramatic moments that spring from the cause-and-effect sequence of action in a scene, you will be able to see right on the script how these moments are placed like stepping stones across a running creek—stones that will take you where you need to go directly and dramatically. This journey, or arc, is also likely to be exciting and economical if you build your acting choices in accordance with the visual that the boxing gives you.

As you begin the rehearsal process on your feet, you can also add any specific blocking you come up with or discover as you work together on your scores.

What follows is an example of how a portion of a scored scene might look. This sample is not intended to be read as the definitive way to break down the scene. There may be literally hundreds of better interpretations. Feel free to take apart and improve the following excerpt. The score is from the point of view of the actor playing Kath.

All of the circled new pieces of info represent major reaction potential for Kath, and had the cutting represented the entire play, each circle of new info might have qualified for a box, as well. But because we are at the beginning of the play, I chose to note them only as good opportunities for making moments. If each good chunk of info were considered a major plot progresser, then there would be far too many stones in the creek to choose from, and they would no longer be helpful in isolating the road map of the action.

Note that, like much of this work, selecting the major dramatic moments for boxing may be very subjective. Although my scoring covered only the opening beats of the script, I still came up with what I considered three major stepping stones in the cause-and-effect journey of the action. I selected the "why don't you gos" because they represent major points of conflict that ultimately propel the story forward. Kath's disdain for Danny at the end of the cutting is also an important action moment, because Danny realizes he is caught in a bind here and chooses to change the direction of the discussion by taking a new tack in the next beat. Although the manhood accusations by Kath are important, they are not yet dealt with in a meaningful way. For that reason, I chose not to box them at this point in the action. All of my choices are up for discussion, however, and it is important to keep in mind that scoring is not about being right or wrong. The scoring is intended only as an aid to help an individual actor find his or her way through the script

Objective: To make Danny deal with the problems outside

Tactic: To get Danny's attention

KATH: What was that?

DANNY: Hunh?

KATH: I heard something.

DANNY: What did it sound…

KATH: Shhh.

DANNY: OK.

Discovery: Hear noise before speaking. Try to determine source of noise.

Physical Action: Shake Danny to get his attention.

Tactic: To give Danny useful information

KATH: It's stopped.

DANNY: Good.

Discovery: Listen for noise.

Physcial Action: Sit up and sit frozen to listen better.

Tactic: To make Danny go investigate

KATH: Go look.

DANNY: What?

KATH: Go look outside. Around the tent.

DANNY: What for?

KATH: It might be something

DANNY: Kath…

KATH: Please.

Find Idea: Determine that I am safe for the moment and decide Danny should investigate.

Physical Action: grab Danny's hand affectionately.

To convince Danny that being dressed does not matter

DANNY: I'm not dressed.

KATH: Who's going to see you?

DANNY: Whatever made the noise.

KATH: It won't care if you have clothes on.

DANNY: It? What kind of it?

Discovery: Danny will not willingly play man's macho role.

Discovery: Realize choice of word "it" creates fear in Danny.

To avoid Danny's Concern about what "it" might be

KATH: I don't know

DANNY: You mean like a bear?

KATH: No. Not necessarily.

Physical Action: Turn away to avoid eye contact.

DANNY: You want me to go look for something that's not necessarily a bear. In the middle of the night. In the middle of nowhere. In my underwear.

KATH: Take the flashlight.

DANNY: Why don't you go?

Physcial Action: Search in dark for flashlight. Find flashlight.

To make Danny go by attacking his manhood

KATH: You're the man.

DANNY: Right. I forgot.

KATH: I was kidding.

Defeat: Realize Danny was scared as I am and won't go easily.

DANNY: No gun, no knife. But I've got the dick. What am I going to do with that? Piss on him? Fuck him?

KATH: You are gross.

DANNY: Thank you.

Physical Action: Sit up facing Danny. Make and keep eye contact to make sure he feels attack on his manhood.

KATH: I was only kidding anyway—about you being the man.

DANNY: Why don't you go?

KATH: Me?

Physical Action: Point to self to demonstrate surprise and shock at suggestion.

DANNY: Yeah, stuff the flashlight in your jeans. The bear will think you're *really* dangerous.

KATH: You are disgusting. Just forget it.

Physical Action: Wave hand dismissindly at Danny to show distain for him.

[*Beat.*]

with economy and effectiveness. Clearly, you are free to interpret the script and score it in the way that is individually most helpful—as long as the story gets told in the clearest, most compelling way possible.

You might want to consider working through this and several other short plays until you get the hang of scoring. You might also read this or another short play and score your script from the point of view of one or more characters. Then you might want to find someone to read with you and practice reading from the script using your notations. By doing so, you will probably make great headway into the analysis and scoring process as well as learn to read effectively from a script. It is very likely that before too long, you will discover that doing the scoring work honestly and completely makes you a better and more efficient actor. In addition, you are likely to discover that you are able to produce more interesting, more exciting, and more believable work in a shorter amount of time than you could previously. You will also be learning a process that, when followed diligently, can provide you with a means to create first-class work with dependability. In other words, you will be developing what every working actor wants desperately to possess—a technique that will serve you in any scripted acting situation.

PART 2
SCENE STUDY

SEVEN

THE VALUE OF SCENE STUDY CLASS

NOT SO LONG AGO, I HAD THE OPPORTUNITY TO WATCH one of my favorite senior acting students take on the title role in Anouilh's *Antigone* as part of our mainstage season. From the time I began teaching her in her freshman year, I felt this young woman to be the most gifted natural actor in the class. But this was to be her first major role in a nonmusical. Up to this point, her dramatic skills were one of the best-kept secrets in the department. At one time early in her sophomore year, I even had to defend retaining her in our program, so her upcoming lead was giving me a great sense of satisfaction. The anticipation of the moment when the rest of the school community would finally discover what I had known for so long was driving me crazy, and I was fully prepared to be blown away by what I saw. Unfortunately, it never worked out quite the way I had planned.

In case you're not familiar with it, Anouilh's version of Sophocles' *Antigone* was written during the Nazi occupation of France, early in the days of World War II, and Anouilh boldly reset his own *Antigone* in the political climate of the time. Though the heart of the play remained essentially the same as the Sophocles version, Anouilh was able to make many subtle and some not-so-subtle analogies between the original mythical setting of ancient Thebes and the occupied France Anouilh inhabited. But the spirit of and heart of *Antigone* remains the same in both versions.

The eponymous heroine of the play is Antigone. If the play is to work effectively, the audience must love, admire, respect, and most importantly root for its hero, in spite of the fact that most who see the play already know its tragic outcome. That, after all, is the nature of tragedy. Further, in the Anouilh version, the character of King Creon is far more sympathetic than in the Sophocles version and tries very hard to save Antigone from the destiny she refuses to avoid. The conflict between these two characters, based the issues of state versus family and civil versus moral law, reflects very accurately the plight of those who ruled Vichy France. The contemporary French audience watching back then would no doubt be forced to take a more objective look at the decisions and politics affecting people at the time. But the one thing that never wavers in either version is Antigone's commitment to her beliefs. It gives her strength over her fears and allows her to enjoy the beauty of her last moments on Earth. It is this inner strength and peace that make her so heroic. It is this peace and calm that give the character such power to move an audience.

In the production I saw, the setting had been changed to some netherworld, a place that combined elements of the medieval, futuristic, and ancient Greek, creating an anachronistic setting that was more anarchic than enlightening and in turn caused the specific references to the 1940s to be either lost completely or, at the least, confused. Further, in this version, because Creon's ethical conflict is disassociated from the specifics of Vichy France, it remained vague and almost irrelevant. But more importantly, in the production I saw, Antigone was portrayed as a whiny girl, locked into a decision that she really didn't want to be making. Though I couldn't have been rooting more for an actor, at the end of the play I was still totally unmoved—by the play and, more to the point, by the character of Antigone and the actor playing her. That my talented young actor came off this way was the only real tragedy I watched that evening.

Of course, in some ways my student can't be blamed for any of this. But in the final judgment, it remains she who is weighed, judged, and criticized. Every actor is ultimately the product or victim of the director and the combined production elements that surround her. And the fact is that many of those who saw her work thought my acting student did an excellent job. But it is also true that a significant part of the audience left the theatre either unmoved or not clear about the point of the whole play, a play that has been making valid comments on the human condition for more than two thousand years.

All things considered, my student did fine. But I know she could have been so much better, not because her director let her down, but because she had the craft to do better in spite of her director's shortcomings. That, of course, is the lesson of this lengthy opening narrative.

WHY SCENE STUDY?

The most effective way to learn your craft is either OJT (on-job training) or through scene study work. No amount of exercises, improvisation, or theatre games can do for you what going through the process of analyzing, synthesizing, blocking, and working a scene can and will do—especially if you have a good teacher. The fact is that no actor is director-proof, unless you are able to do for yourself what too many actors expect the director to do. A good acting teacher should be giving you the craft to be able to do for yourself so that you are never a victim to the failings of a director or a misconceived production. Scene study provides the best arena for this training.

From earlier chapters, you already know that I have come to define good acting as acting that is believable and tells the best possible story while serving the script. In other words, regardless of the world of the play, the audience must believe the characters they are watching. But it is up to the actor to make choices that are as interesting as possible while supporting the intention of that script. In the example of the production of *Antigone,* the world of the play was never well defined, so a reference to a cigarette, a foxtrot, and a black limousine juxtaposed with a discussion about Greek burial rites could be both confusing and off-putting. An argument about whether a young girl should live or die because of allegiance to state or God should never be less than what it is—a life-and-death discussion that should keep the characters and the audience riveted and involved. And a play about a tragic hero must have a character whose choices make the audience empathize to the point of catharsis, or the tragic elements written into the play are not being served.

A good play, a timeless play, a play that stays around for two thousand years stays around that long because it works. When an actor makes choices that serve the play, the actor can't help but stay on track, and the play becomes far easier to act. When the actor understands what is going on in the play, the moments move smoothly from one to another and everything makes sense with little effort or struggle. On the other hand, when an actor counters the choices that are built into the script, he plays a risky game, in which either he succeeds at the expense of the play, or all involved go down together.

And so an effective scene study class is not just about memorizing lines and moving around onstage until you are comfortable. Nor is it simply about finding your deepest and truest emotions. Rather, it is about analyzing the script independently, coming together with a scene partner and finding common ground, developing together the arc of the scene, finding the blocking that best serves the story being told, and working the moments, the beats, and then the overall scene until each moment flows into the next. This will happen eventually—because as actors, you will have done your homework so efficiently and effectively through the rehearsal process that by the time of the final presentation, you will be totally listening and reacting to each other moment by moment, creating for the audience the illusion that it is all happening for the first time.

PARTNERING

Off the top of your head, you might think the beginning of the scene study process comes with the selection of material. But actually, it doesn't. Selecting the right partner can be just as important as the material you select, and it probably should come first. The question is, when you pick a scene partner, are you doing so for reasons related to your acting development, or for social ones? Is it because you want to work with someone to get to know her better, or is it because you want to work with the best actor in the class, who will challenge you and help you grow? Maybe you choose to work with someone who has a similar schedule that will make for easy-to-get-together rehearsal time, or maybe you don't consider availability at all when making your partnering choices. Obviously, you get the point I'm trying to make.

Though it is nice for friends to get to work together, it is important for you to remember that doing theatre is a collaborative art, which does not necessarily mean that everyone who works together must love each other. It is important that you learn the skill of working together with all kinds of people whether you like them or not—because that is what you will have to do in the real world of theatre and, for that matter, in life. Besides, you should consider the rehearsal process a matter of business as much as fun. It is your business to be able to get the job done, whether the situation is ideal or not.

There has been an underlying assumption here, one that needs to be stated specifically. So here goes. Scene work should involve only two actors. Scene-work anthologies consist primarily of two-character scenes, and certainly most scene study classes run on that basis. The fact is, hands down, the two-character scene is the best way to go. Playwrights know that a strong conflict between two characters is the easiest for them to handle, and the vast majority of scenes with a clear throughline of action best suited for classroom or studio work are of the two-character variety. As each additional character is placed into the framework of a scene, the difficulty establishing and playing conflict, as well as maintaining a clear arc in the storyline, increases exponentially. Why choose to complicate a process that is already difficult in terms of both analysis and execution? Besides, the more actors you place into an interpersonal dynamic, the more difficult the process becomes. It's hard enough to make it work with one scene partner; why add to the burden?

SELECTING THE SCENE

Well-selected material means challenging work that can help you focus on acting problems specific to your needs. If you don't know what your greatest needs are, your teacher, if she is a good one, will soon let you know. As you hear the same kinds of things repeated to you, you will begin to understand what you should be looking for in a scene. In the beginning of a scene study class, if you don't know what you should be looking for in a scene, find one that is straightforward, with a strong, clear conflict to play. Stick with something that gives you a character that is within your reach. Playing age or someone that is nothing like who you are is liable to get in the way of working on your basic believability and compellingness. As you begin to understand your strengths and weaknesses, you can start to tailor your choices in a more efficient way, or your teacher will be able to make recommendations appropriate for you.

Another assumption I have been making is that you read plays on a regular basis. If you call yourself an actor, I would assume you do. If that is not the case, you should be reading them all the time, working on your analysis skills and general body of dramatic knowledge. You should be collecting scenes that will be good for you to work on as you accumulate the number of plays you have read. Keep a list, or put scenes in a folder that you keep for that purpose.

Over the years, I have built up an enormous repertoire of plays and authors that I have discovered work exceptionally well with my students and that cover the myriad problems that my young actors should be working on. Below you will find a list of plays that have been effective with the students in my classes. Perhaps you may find it useful, as well.

SUGGESTED PLAYS

Accelerando Lisa Loomer

Agnes of God John Pielmeier

Ah, Wilderness! Eugene O'Neill

Album David Rimmer

All My Sons Arthur Miller

The Altruists Nicky Silver

Am I Blue Beth Henley

Amber Waves James Still

And Miss Reardon Drinks a Little Paul Zindel

Angels in America Tony Kushner

Animals and Plants Adam Rapp

Apartment 3A Jeff Daniels

As Bees in Honey Drown Douglas Carter Beane

Ascension Day Timothy Mason

Aunt Dan and Lemon Wallace Shawn

Awake and Sing! Clifford Odets

Baby with the Bathwater Christopher Durang

Bad Seed Maxwell Anderson

The Baltimore Waltz Paula Vogel

Barefoot in the Park Neil Simon

Be Aggressive Annie Weisman

Betrayal Harold Pinter

Betty's Summer Vacation Christopher Durang

Beyond Therapy Christopher Durang

Biloxi Blues Neil Simon

Birdbath Leonard Melfi

Blood Knot Athol Fugard

Blue Surge Rebecca Gilman

Blue Window Craig Lucas

Boom Town Jeff Daniels

Boy Julia Jordan

Boy Gets Girl Rebecca Gilman

Boys' Life Howard Korder

Brighton Beach Memoirs Neil Simon

Broadway Bound Neil Simon

Brooklyn Boy Donald Margulies

Bug Tracy Letts

The Butterfly Collection Theresa Rebeck

The Children's Hour Lillian Hellman

Coastal Disturbances Tina Howe

Come Back, Little Sheba William Inge

Come Back to the 5 and Dime… Ed Graczyk

The Conduct of Life Maria Irene Fornes

A Coupla White Chicks… John Ford Noonan

Crimes of the Heart Beth Henley

The Crucible Arthur Miller

Curse of the Starving Class Sam Shepard

Danny and the Deep Blue Sea John Patrick Shanley

Dark at the Top of the Stairs William Inge

The Day They Shot John Lennon James McLure

The Days and Nights of Beebee Fenstermaker William Snyder

Death and the Maiden Ariel Dorfman

Death of a Salesman Arthur Miller

The Death of Bessie Smith Edward Albee

Dinner with Friends Donald Margulies

The Distance from Here Neil LaBute

The Dumb Waiter Harold Pinter

Eastern Standard Richard Greenberg

Educating Rita Willy Russell

The Effect of Gamma Rays on Man-in-the-Moon Marigolds Paul Zindel

Eleemosynary Lee Blessing

The Family of Mann Theresa Rebeck

Fat Men in Skirts Nicky Silver

Fat Pig Neil LaBute

Faulkner's Bicycle Heather McDonald

Fences August Wilson

Fifth of July Lanford Wilson

The Film Society Jon Robin Baitz

Final Placement Ara Watson

Fit to Be Tied Nicky Silver

Five Women Wearing the Same Dress Alan Ball

The Food Chain Nicky Silver

Fool for Love Sam Shepard

For Colored Girls Who Have Considered… Ntozake Shange

Frozen Bryony Lavery

Fuddy Meers David Lindsay-Abaire

Getting Out Marsha Norman

The Gingerbread Lady Neil Simon

The Glass Menagerie Tennessee Williams

The Goat Edward Albee

Greater Tuna Ed Howard, Joe Sears, and Jaston Williams

A Hatful of Rain Michael Gazzo

Hello from Bertha Tennessee Williams

Hold Please Annie Weisman

Hooters Ted Tally

The House of Blue Leaves John Guare

I Hate Hamlet Paul Rudnick

I Remember Mama John Van Druten

Impossible Marriage Beth Henley

Independence Lee Blessing

Our Country's Good
Timberlake Wertenbaker

Our Town Thornton Wilder

Out of Gas on Lovers Leap
Mark St. Germain

A Perfect Ganesh Terrence McNally

The Piano Lesson August Wilson

Picnic William Inge

Popcorn Ben Elton

Porch Jeffrey Sweet

Proof David Auburn

Pterodactyls Nicky Silver

Rabbit Hole David Lindsay-Abaire

Raised in Captivity Nicky Silver

Reckless Craig Lucas

Red Light Winter Adam Rapp

Refuge Jessica Goldberg

The Rimers of Eldritch Lanford Wilson

The Rise and Rise of Daniel Rocket
Peter Parnell

Sarita Maria Irene Fornes

Savage in Limbo John Patrick Shanley

The Sea Horse Edward Moore

Search and Destroy Howard Korder

Seven Guitars August Wilson

The Shape of Things Neil LaBute

Shivaree William Mastrosimone

Sin Wendy MacLeod

The Sisters Rosensweig
Wendy Wasserstein

Snakebit David Marshall Grant

Some Girls Neil LaBute

Someone Who'll Watch Over Me
Frank McGuinness

Speed the Plow David Mamet

Spike Heels Theresa Rebeck

Spinning into Butter Rebecca Gilman

Spring Awakening Frank Wedekind,
trans. Edward Bond

St. Scarlet Julia Jordan

Steaming Nell Dunn

Steel Magnolias Robert Harling

The Stonewater Rapture Doug Wright

Stop Kiss Diana Son

Streamers David Rabe

A Streetcar Named Desire
Tennessee Williams

The Strong Breed Wole Soyinka

The Substance of Fire Jon Robin Baitz

The Sum of Us David Stevens

Sylvia A. R. Gurney

A Taste of Honey Shelagh Delaney

This Is Our Youth Kenneth Lonergan

Three Days of Rain Richard Greenberg

Top Dog/Underdog Suzan-Lori Parks

Top Girls Caryl Churchill

Two Rooms Lee Blessing

Uncommon Women and Others
Wendy Wasserstein

The Value of Names Jeffrey Sweet

Vanishing Act Richard Greenberg

Veins and Thumbtacks
Jonathan Marc Sherman

The Wager Mark Medoff

A Walk in the Woods Lee Blessing

The Water Children Wendy MacLeod

Weekend Near Madison Kathleen Tolan

Who's Afraid of Virginia Woolf?
Edward Albee

The Widow Claire Horton Foote

Wit Margaret Edson

With and Without Jeffrey Sweet

Women and Wallace
Jonathan Marc Sherman

Wonder of the World
David Lindsay-Abaire

The Woolgatherer
William Mastrosimone

The Zoo Story Edward Albee

This list, of course, is meant as a starting point. For every play I've named here there are probably a hundred that I should have included, and most of the authors listed here have written many other worthy plays that would be useful in a scene study class. But from each of the plays listed here, I have seen worthwhile scenes worked on in my classes. Scenes that have provided the raw material for growth in the actors working on them. In most cases, the scenes are age-appropriate for young actors, or the differences in age between the characters and the actors playing them still offer more benefit than obstacle to the actors employing them. Some of the material, however, may not be appropriate for all classrooms. Be sure that you have consulted with your teacher before embarking on a play that won't be acceptable for a particular classroom setting.

I still find it daunting when new scenes are starting in my classes and I am surrounded by students calling out for me to instantly offer up the perfect suggestions. "Comedies!" "Something dramatic for me and Liz." "We want to do a love scene, something real gushy!" My usual response is to tell my students to back off, and then I take some time with the names of partners to compose a list of two or three suggestions for each pairing. But this should not really be your teacher's responsibility. It is yours.

As an actor you should want to be reading scripts, as many as possible, as often as you can. It will help you grow. You should also be reading those plays in a practical, actor-effective way. Passive reading is not a practical way for you to try to find material. You should be reading actively—always asking questions about what is happening in the action, how the play works, the cause-and-effect nature of the events the characters go through, and all the other "basic elements of drama." If you don't develop the habit of reading potential dramatic material in this way, more often than not you are likely to pass over excellent plays and scenes simply because you are unable to recognize their potential.

I can remember back to my early days of searching for a good scene to work on. How often would I reject something only to discover later, when someone else was doing it, how great a scene I had chosen to eighty-six. I had been reading like an English major, perhaps, but not like an actor.

Remember, it takes time and energy to analyze, memorize, and block a scene. But the process should be an exciting one, filled with challenges and discoveries. If you are already bored with the material you have selected before you get to the point where you understand it enough to make significant in-the-moment discoveries, you are doing something wrong. You have to be sure that the material you have selected will provide the right platform. The rehearsal process should be energizing all the way through. Otherwise, you'll find yourself turning to a new scene and be forced to start the process all over without getting the satisfaction of truly feeling like an actor. A scene should continue to grow at each stage of the process. Consider it like a marriage between you and your partner, and the material. You wouldn't want to marry just anybody. So be sure before you give each other the ring and set your date.

One of the most popular ways to find scenes comes from the use of those scene study collections that fill the shelves in the drama sections of most well-stocked bookstores and possibly your shelves at home. These are great insofar as you have at your fingertips prechosen scenes from good plays. By good, I mean plays that work dramatically when performed onstage. We are not necessarily talking about great dramatic literature here; we are talking about plays that have been written by playwrights who understand how to write effectively using conflict—the engine of drama. In turn, the editors have chosen these particular scenes because they know the plays and scenes work, at least on the printed page, or potentially when performed. Many of these scenes will work well for you once you understand what the words on the printed page have to offer.

Now the question about reading the entire play needs be addressed. It is a given that any scene from a play must be considered in the context in which it appears in that play. A scene taken from a play comes after the previous action in that play, and before the action that follows. An understanding of the given circumstances of the particular moment in which the scene takes place is absolutely critical to making the scene work. The summaries provided in most scene study books are simply inadequate, certainly if you're a beginning actor, for finding the specifics of the circumstances of the play and scene to be worked on. When you as an actor can't enter the scene with the necessary understanding, you may simply be unable to make it work, because you don't have enough information to make good choices.

Some scene anthologies, like the recent *Duo,* for instance, claim that the selected scenes can stand on their own, out of the context of the play they come from. This may be true, and for some work your teacher may want to have you consider a particular scene out of context just to focus you on making choices that allow a scene to work, without considering the given circumstances of the overall play. But generally, I am not in favor of this approach. One of the hardest things for actors to do, in my opinion, is to make good choices—choices that spring from a careful analysis of the scene in context, choices that make the scene work, yes, but also contribute to the overall flow of the script. If you skip this part of the process and focus only on making a scene work out of context, I fear you might be encouraged to disregard your overall obligation to tell the entire story in a compelling and clear way.

Ultimately, it is the job of working actors to put themselves in the situation of dealing with an entire play and face the traps and pitfalls every play contains. That said, beginning actors sometimes think it is their responsibility to tell the entire story of the play while working on their scene. Since the classroom audience may not know all that came before and all that will come after, they feel it their obligation to retell the entire story of the play in the scene. Avoid this. You must learn to make choices in a scene that reflect what the characters you are playing know at that particular time. It is so tempting to play a scene with what you know about your character from a reading of the entire play, putting in knowledge and understanding that your character does not yet have because their journey in the play has not taken them to that place yet. Since ultimately, it is your purpose with scene study to learn how to survive the rehearsal process of a play, or make choices that reflect the out-of-sequence shooting schedule of a film, it seems critical that you reinforce for yourself the notion that what happens onstage happens in a particular and very specific context.

Now that we have gotten through the philosophical aspects of choosing material, let's return to a discussion of the selection process as it regards your specific acting needs. Here are some examples of the kinds of acting problems you might still currently face. Each problem is followed by a scene quality that might help you work on that particular problem.

Believable onstage, but can't make the story clear for an audience—a simple, clear-cut, cause-and-effect scene—one in which discoveries or new information arises continuously.

Inability to make big and compelling choices—a scene that is a climax from a play.

Makes everything big, but nothing seems real—a scene in which the actor must strongly need something from the acting partner; a nonclimactic scene.

Doesn't listen onstage, acts in a vacuum—a scene that requires mostly reacting to the acting partner.

Cannot look at or touch scene partner—a scene that requires eye contact and intimacy.

Acts only from the neck up—scenes with little dialogue and requiring a lot of physical action.

Cannot physically use space or set effectively—a scene set in a realistic space where dialogue comes out of believable ongoing business, such as cleaning up after a meal.

Cannot play an objective—a scene that has an obvious, single, clear conflict.

Cannot play the positive (pursuing an objective in a way that is likely to get it)—an argument or discussion-of-an-issue scene.

Cannot do one thing at a time—a scene with a simple, clear-cut objective to play and a step-by-step progression.

Does not finish an action—a scene where what is done physically is more important than the dialogue.

Focuses only on spoken dialogue, not on action of story underlining dialogue—a scene where the actor does more listening yet has a big arc or throughline to travel during the scene.

Emphasizes the wrong words when saying dialogue—a scene where most of the dialogue is in reaction to what is said.

Cannot color words to make them specific and personal—a scene that contains dialogue consisting of lists.

Cannot distinguish between what is important and what is not—a conversation scene.

Cannot memorize, or cannot memorize accurately—a scene in which physical action is as important as dialogue.

As you learn to think in this way, your categories of problems, as well as your library of possible solution scenes, will develop over time.

CHOOSING A CUTTING

It is probably a mistake to do scenes that are longer than five minutes. To make five minutes' worth of material work takes an enormous amount of time, energy, and thought. By establishing that time limit for yourself at the beginning, and sticking to it, you can ensure that you put your time and energy into what is most important.

What you want in a scene is a clear-cut developmental sequence. Since the playwright knows that conflict is the engine of drama, consciously or not, that playwright develops on the printed page a situation in which each character needs something from the other and pursues that purpose or *objective* in the scene. *Obstacles* and resistance that will make the scene interesting to work on and watch will be built in. It is the progression of the scene—its arc or throughline—however, moment to moment, that really makes any scene come alive, from the discovery of the problem, to the development of the conflict, to the strategic maneuverings of the characters to fulfill their needs and resolve that problem. This sequence unfolds brick by brick—one *moment,* one *beat,* at a time. Each new moment is built from the previous one, and unless you learn to respect this fact, you will never find out what is contained in each moment and learn to develop the next moment from the previous one.

In spite of my saying all this, you will probably want to do entire scenes. It will give you a sense of closure. It will make you feel like you have gone through an entire little play with your scene partner. Unfortunately, scenes from which you can immediately feel this way are usually more than five minutes long. And unfortunately, when you tackle more than five minutes of material, it ends up being too much to work on. Because you'll probably have a limited time to rehearse and you'll feel that you must cover the whole scene, you'll end up not working moment to moment. Invariably, you and your partner will run the whole scene without stopping and then ask each other, "How was it for you that time through?," discuss a few notes, and simply run the whole scene again. This rehearsal approach ends up reinforcing exactly the opposite of what you should be focusing on.

I suggest that you be very firm with yourself about the five-minutes-or-less rule. Your scene does not have to start at the beginning of the actual scene to make it an effective learning device, nor does it have to go to the end. What is important is developing the arc of the scene a moment at a time. If you just ice-skate through a scene—simply run through it from beginning to end—you will never learn the importance of making moments, you will never learn to connect with your scene partner, and you will never learn to listen and react effectively. You must continually work toward these goals. By sticking with the five-minute rule, you will learn to prioritize effectively and work brick by brick.

A note for clarity here. Scenes should not be cut internally in order to keep them to five minutes. Skip several beats at the beginning of a scene, or stop several beats before the end, but do not mess with the structure the playwright has created. If you cut the scene internally, you might destroy sequential links that are absolutely necessary for making the scene work dramatically. You must always assume that since the scene selected is from a good play written by a skilled playwright, everything in the scene is there for a reason—even if you don't at the beginning of the process know what that reason is.

CHAPTER EIGHT

THE ACTOR'S HOMEWORK

ALL RIGHT, YOUR PARTNERSHIP IS MADE, AND THE SCENE is selected, and you have done your initial homework. Now what happens? I suggest that before you run off to rehearse, you start with some rules that will provide you with an understanding about the process and about the product you will produce. Here follow some excerpts from the guidelines I use in my class. They may prove helpful in your analysis of what a successful scene collaboration will entail.

- Scene study is a partnership; make it work.
- If one partner screws up, you go down together.
- You will treat your partner with respect.
- You will be treated by your teacher as adult professionals. It is your responsibility to act as such.
- You are responsible for making and keeping rehearsal appointments.
- You are expected to be prepared on the day your work is to be put up.
- The time you spend in preparation depends on the time you need in order to come in prepared.
- Prepared means meeting the obligations of the scene to the best of your ability.
- No excuses, just the work.

- Your ability or inability to memorize is your personal problem or burden. No special treatment because it takes you longer. Being prepared is part of the game.
- Discuss all given circumstances and agree on what they are. Do not discuss your objectives, just play them.
- Don't direct your scene partner.
- The focus of the work is process, not product. Improvement, not perfection, is the goal.
- Learning something new is more important than getting it right.
- Criticism is medicine. Learn to love taking it.
- An actor learns more from fixing mistakes than by getting praise.
- Criticism must focus more on what is not working than what is.
- Don't try to prove you're right; it's a waste of time.
- You act for an audience; make it work for them.
- Your audience is usually right.
- Don't waste energy trying to convince your audience that they are wrong. It only makes things worse.
- The goal of going through the scene study process is not to produce a perfect scene, but rather, to practice working through the various steps in the process and, through practice, get better at each.
- Don't judge yourself on the work of the day. Look at the growth pattern.
- You learn more from working than watching. Prepare the work, work often, and grow.
- If your work is not prepared, don't waste the class's time. Preparation and responsibility are as important as any other aspect of the process of acting. Your work ethic affects everyone else in theatre.

I always allow my students to decide for themselves when they will work in class. They know their schedules and obligations better than I do, so I trust that they will make better decisions than I will. However, once they commit to a presentation time, I hold them to it. One of the biggest crimes a student can commit in an acting class is not putting up on the scheduled day and leaving me with a hole to fill. Someone else could have been working. Sometimes a life emergency does occur, but you should be responsible for getting a replacement team to go instead of you. Your work ethic in theatre is vital. If you commit to putting up your work at a particular time, make sure that you do it. And make sure you are doing the best work you possibly can.

How often should you be able to put up your work? Obviously, the answer depends on the size of your class, the amount of time you have per session, and the amount of time your teacher spends on each scene. Since the variables may be tremendous, I'll just offer up the following. Working often is essential to the forward progress of a scene. It is human nature to delay working until later rather than sooner. But if you wait too long between put-ups, you will either forget the essential commentary from the previous showing or end up remembering inaccurately, and then focus on the wrong things in your next set of rehearsals with your partner. Don't wait too long after a put-up to work the scene again with your partner. That way the notes received will still be clear and fresh.

Remember, your preparation for a scene begins with your homework—the independent analysis you do before meeting with your partner. Your analysis should follow the guidelines set up in the previous chapters. For convenience, I will repeat the scene study preparation questions listed earlier.

1. Describe the given circumstances of the scene based on your reading of the entire play.

2. What is the story of the scene? Literally, what are the story events one by one in a cause-and-effect fashion?

3. What is/are the conflicts in the scene that make the scene work?

4. What are the most dramatic moments in the scene? Why? How does the script build to these moments? Be specific.

5. What is the climax of the scene? Justify.

6. How does your character contribute to the conflict in the scene?

7. What does your character need (objective) in this scene from the other character?

8. What are the actions your character actually performs in the scene? Literally list the things he/she does—physically and psychologically.

9. What prevents your character from getting what is needed?

10. What does your character do to get around these obstacles?

11. How badly does your character need what is needed?

12. What is your character willing to do to get what is needed?

13. What discoveries does your character make during the scene?

14. How does this new information change your character? Does it change your character's behavior, way of thinking, needs?

15. Identify the places in the script where new information is received by your character.

16. How does this information change what your character thinks and/or feels? Does this news signal a victory? A defeat? A change in the way the character deals?

17. What internal changes does your character go through at these moments?

18. Score the throughline of action for your character based on your answers to the above questions.

I refer to the first presentation of work as *the first read* because I allow my students to do the scene with their scripts in hand. (Some teachers do not work this way. They may want you memorized for the first presentation. Others may simply ask you to read the scene without having asked you to come prepared with choices based on a detailed analysis and having rehearsed.) But in my class, the first read is not a cold one. It is totally prepared. The first read is a presentation that will reflect the actors' understanding of the scene overall and moment by moment.

I expect my actors to be listening, reacting, and fulfilling their objectives. They should be making discoveries, playing off the new information, and adjusting to their victories and defeats. That means that though the words are not completely memorized, the actors will know the action of the scene moment by moment and will know the dialogue well enough that they can listen to and look at each other at almost all times. Only when they are about to speak should they need to look down at their scripts to get the next line. And they know their scripts well enough that a simple quick glance will allow them to return to eye contact with their scene partner immediately.

The only significant difference between what is required here, and what will be required the next time up, is the blocking and memorization. My actors can remain seated for the first read and, by doing so, will not yet have the burden of acting the scene physically. This lack of blocking, however, does not mean that my actors can ignore things that happen physically. They must accommodate for any physical action that does occur in the scene. Otherwise, their acting choices and use of dialogue will not make sense. If moving believably and reading is too much for you to juggle, I strongly suggest you try following this procedure just described.

Before going off to rehearse, just a reminder. Even though you are doing only one scene from the play, as discussed earlier, you should not take on the obligation to summarize the whole play in this scene. In other words, your choices for the scene should be no different than if you were doing the whole play. You should not try to make choices to convey information that would have been brought out elsewhere and that may be necessary for the audience's understanding of the overall story. This kind of information can be explained to your class before you begin your scene. You should rehearse the scene making the same choices you would make if you had just completed the previous scene in the context of the play.

THE SCENE WORK PROCESS—AN OVERVIEW

I THINK OF MYSELF AS A TEACHING DIRECTOR. I CONSIDER it part of my responsibility to teach my students how to work independently during the rehearsal process. I try to avoid, sometimes at much cost, simply giving them choices, moves, and actions that will make them look brilliant. Yes, of course I want them to look good in performance. That's part of my job. When they look good, the whole production profits—the play works, I come off like I know what I'm doing, and my students seem be as talented as I know they are.

But I also want my students to learn to work without a director's help. Therefore, whenever possible in the rehearsal process, I try to get my young actors to think through what they are doing at any particular moment onstage, so they can make choices that will serve the scene and the overall story their characters are playing out. Of course, I am limited by time pressures and by each student's ability to make effective choices economically, so there always comes a point when I must give the actors, to some degree, what is needed in the scene. I do this because it is my responsibility to make the whole play work and I must have what is needed at that point, for the overall good of the production. But I will almost never do that when I am teaching in class. As a teacher, I want my students to learn how to find the choices for themselves. They learn more when they are forced to find answers on their own, and ultimately, they develop skills that allow them to work well in spite of whether a director is helping them or not.

Many theatre directors don't work this way, of course, and many directors, even many who are considered fine directors, are not particularly good at working with actors. In film this is even more the case. Many movie directors come from the film school rather than the theatre department, and their background is in shooting movies, not in understanding script dynamics and getting what they need from actors. In fact, it is not unusual for these film directors to look to the actors they hire to provide them with the dramatic insights that will help them make their films work for an audience. Remember, well-budgeted films give directors the luxury of doing take after take until they like what they see.

In a scene study class, no time pressures force actors into getting to the right choices as quickly as possible, so there is no need for a director to give you answers. The purpose of a scene study class is to help you develop the skills that will enable you to independently make choices that work and convert these choices into effective actions onstage. Your objective in scene study should be to develop your ability to move, talk, listen, and react in such a way that the script you are working from not only becomes clear and compelling for an audience, but, when combined with what you bring to it, becomes something even greater.

Therefore, what you want ideally in an acting class is a teacher who will develop your skills, not give you the answers that will make you look good. You want a class that will help you learn to become director-proof. The acting teacher you want to work with is one who is looking to make you a better independent actor—that is, an actor who can bring the goods to the table, not one who can look good with the proper manipulation. That means you want someone who will not provide you with solutions to your immediate acting problems, nor tell you how to do a particular moment. This kind of help will not make you a better actor. It will only make you look better at that particular moment. Look for an acting teacher who will provide you with the tools and technique to find those solutions for yourself. In other words, acting teachers are not the same as directors.

Acting teachers should not be directors, in fact. Directors want results and will give answers to get those results. Acting teachers, one the other hand, want very different results—results that, more often than not, are long-term rather than short-term. I have studied with more than a few acting teachers who simply directed scenes in the classroom. It always felt wonderful when the good director offered a few suggestions and turned a failing scene around with a magical comment or two. "When you start that line, try staying at the desk, and don't approach your scene partner until you get to the line…" With a single comment, an awkward, ineffectual moment would suddenly become the catalyst for the fight that my scene partner and I couldn't generate previously no matter what. What satisfaction, what triumph! What an actor I had suddenly become! But how did the director's eye help me learn to do that for myself once I was working without her? The answer is it didn't.

What you want is a teacher who will react to your work from the audience's point of view and share with you from that vantage point what works and what doesn't work in a scene or in a moment; and then, hopefully, the teacher will help you find possible solutions that will be effective. The journey to these acting solutions must be collaborative; you must be involved in the discovery and solution process. Sometimes it will be necessary for your teacher to offer multiple-choice options to you to get you on track, but an effective acting teacher will encourage you to try out those options in front of the class, allowing you to test and analyze the results. Sometimes it might even become necessary to suggest which of the multiple-choice options will work, but you don't want a teacher who will make it all work for you. Finding the solution should be your responsibility. That way you will learn and take a step toward your own mastery.

In the previous chapters, we have talked in some detail about the specific goals of a scene study class. We have discussed methods for selecting partners, scenes, cuttings, and working procedures. We have talked about rules and expectations, and we have reviewed the questions you should be thinking about during your preparation for your first read in class. We also learned what a first read should look like in general terms. Before we get into more detail, however, it might be worthwhile to discuss a plan of action that can be used during the work on a particular scene. I'll go through my overall battle plan in a general way first, and then we'll go back for a more detailed explanation of process.

My sequence goes as follows:

- The first read
- Blocking the scene
- Working the scene
- Last showing

I always begin with a first read of a scene. As I said earlier, this is a prepared reading, not a cold one. You will have read the play and studied the scene. You will have gone through the analysis questions and made choices based on your understanding. You will have shared with your partner your take on the given circumstances and, where necessary, come to agreement on exactly what is happening in the scene. You will have rehearsed with each other, focusing on playing your objectives and listening and reacting to what is being said and done. Though the lines are not necessarily memorized, you will be expected to be familiar enough with what is being said and done that the focus can be on listening rather than on simply reading lines. Just reading lines is unacceptable.

In the first read, I expect that actors are acting. The only thing that does not happen in the first read is movement. There need not be any on-your-feet *blocking*. However, as explained in the previous chapter, any *movement* or *business* suggested by the script must be accounted for in your acting. In other words, if there is a knock at the door, you must acknowledge that knock through your words and actions. Or to put it another way, you must be accounting for all the things that happen in the scene, in spite of the fact that you are freed from the burden of physically enacting it. That comes next.

The next step is blocking. Blocking includes all movement, business, and *gesture*. In scene study class, I focus primarily on the first two items. I expect my actors will have made initial blocking choices and will have begun to include in their work any necessary business that their characters engage in. Gesture is more organic, and in the early stages of rehearsal there is so much to think about that specific gestures appropriate for the characters being played can be considered later. Consider gesture a back-burner item.

Keep in mind that you will not be able to make useful blocking choices unless you have made decisions about the layout of your sets and the set pieces on them. No movements can be made unless you have a place to move from and a place to move to. This need to define the physical space usually proves to be less obvious than it seems. The same is true for business. Useful, grounded stage business is difficult to come by unless you have brought props or, at the least, thought about what props are necessary to make the scene work.

My expectation is that all blocking choices will help make the story, as defined in the first read, more clear and compelling than it was in the previous presentation. Blocking choices should not be about pretty pictures per se;

they should be about making the story clear to the audience. Characters move because they need to; they do business because they need to. All physical actions help define the story and the characters that enact them. The physical actions selected and executed by actors in their scene work are every bit as important as the words they say. My expectation is to see that fact reflected in the thoughtful blocking work my students put up.

In the workthroughs that follow, all notes from the previous put-up are expected to be embraced and accounted for in the newest version of the work. Blocking choices will continue to be revised and refined to accommodate any changes and growth in the work, and all other aspects of the work may change, as well. You will be encouraged to continue to work moment to moment, building the scene a brick at a time.

After the first blocking put-up, some teacher will do two more workthroughs of material, some only one. I have tried it both ways. I always try to weigh the value of what my students learn from doing it again, versus what they will get if they find a new scene and start the whole process from the beginning. The decision always depends on what the students most need for their development at that moment, and that differs from student to student. If I do continue with a particular scene, it is not simply to get the students to master the scene (unless I feel it is important for the student to get to that place), but rather to allow the student to refine and develop some particular skills that the latter part of the scene study process offers. The philosophy, as stated earlier, is always about growth in process, not about producing polished products. You must learn to think that way, as well. Your purpose is to grow, not to look good for the moment.

That, then, is a sequential overview. Now let's examine the process in more detail.

CHAPTER TEN

THE
FIRST READ
IN DETAIL

AS OFTEN AS NOT, AND CERTAINLY THE INITIAL TIME
through a set of first reads, I consider the work I see as totally unsuccessful. Ideally, the first read should make clear the unfolding story of the scene as written, and the actors who are reading the scene should be believable. In a prepared reading for an audition, the actors who get the roles can probably achieve this believability, or better put, those who can achieve it are much more likely to remain in the running for the roles they are up for. The first readings in my acting class would seldom qualify my students for roles. This is not as awful as it sounds. You learn from your mistakes—and, without a doubt, the actors watching the work learn a great deal, as well, particularly from the empirical evidence of seeing the improved version of the scene after I work with my actors. The biggest reasons for the failure rate are twofold. First of all, in most cases, beginning actors fail to focus on making the story of the scene clear and interesting. Second, in spite of repeated warnings from their teacher, student actors tend to focus on a correct reading of the words of the script, rather than on playing their objectives and listening with all their senses to what their acting partners are saying and doing. More on this in a bit.

I begin the first-read process with what I call the "hot seat." Before I would allow you to read the scene you have prepared, I would ask you a series of questions that would allow me to determine whether you have adequately handled your analysis responsibilities. If you have gone through the scene study questions listed in previous chapters, you should be able to handle most of what I ask you. I would be particularly interested in your ability to make clear the story of the scene because, in spite of the lip service you might pay me, your tendency would be to ignore thinking about the story in favor of focusing on character and emotion, two subjects I seldom talk about at this stage of the work. We have already established that emotion is intangible and too hard to play directly. And your character comes from the actions you choose to play and how you would play them, so thinking about inhabiting a character is just plain diving too deep at this point. You should be focusing on craft, not art, particularly at this stage of the game.

The issues I am particularly interested in include the following:

- The given circumstances that set up the scene
- The central conflict of the scene
- The objective of your character—that is, what you need from the other character in the scene
- The story of the scene, event by event
- The biggest, most important moments in the scene

In addition, I always ask the significance of the title of the play, and the story of the play in general. The title often suggests important clues to the meaning and purpose of the play and to the essential storyline. It is therefore worth early consideration. Following that, if I found that you could not articulate the story essentials, I might just think that you have not read the play in its entirety, or you have read it so superficially that your reading hasn't really helped you understand where the scene you are about to do comes from and how it fits in to the overall story sequence of the play.

If your ignorance about the overall story is too obvious, I might refuse to allow you and your partner to proceed into the read. Reading and understanding the overall play is that important, in my opinion—important enough to disallow work. If your responses to other hot-seat questions are inadequate, unjustified, or simply wrong, I might also stop before allowing the scene to be put up. These are judgment calls, of course, and depend on many specific circumstances that may be different for you than for another actor. But whatever your own circumstances, establishing proper work habits is a critical part of the craft you are learning.

The work habits you develop are as important as acting itself. Living up to your potential at all the stages of your training will help you master craft quickly and efficiently. Too many young actors undervalue reading and understanding the material being worked on. Hopefully, at this point in the book, you understand how wrongheaded this attitude is.

I always struggle with the issue of whether or not to make my students write the answers to all the questions they should deal with. Doing so is extremely time-consuming. For my own students time is always an issue, so I fret that if they spend all their time writing the answers to scene study questions they will have less time to actually work on the material, and the resulting presentation will therefore be compromised. On the other hand, at the beginning of the first semester of scene study, when I ask my hot-seat students the important questions, they are often unable to clearly articulate their answers. In some cases, I can tell that the answers are in there somewhere but my students are simply unable to present them verbally. But I also know that there is a high correlation between being able to articulate what you are doing as an actor and being able to do it. In other words, fuzzy speaking equals fuzzy acting. This axiom becomes particularly clear when I ask my actors about their objectives. If you can articulate your purpose simply and clearly, you are much more likely to be able to execute it simply and clearly in the scene you will be reading a few moments after.

The logic so far seems to suggest that, all things considered, it might be a good idea for you to write down your answers. Perhaps. But often what happens when I ask my students to write the answers to all the questions is that the writing becomes too much of a burden after a while. Increasingly, the written answers become rote and careless and eventually become no more useful than the unclear verbal response. I end up reading pages and pages of time-consuming but worthless material. So what's the answer? You'll have to find out what works best for you.

Whether you decide it works best to write the answers to all the questions, it is essential that you make notations on your script—in pencil only, since much of what you think about the scene may change during the rehearsal process (and use only a photocopy of the script—no writing in actual scripts unless you own them). These notations, as demonstrated in the script-analysis chapter, would include beat changes; objectives and tactics; transitional moments; where victories, defeats, and discoveries occur; and operative words. When these kinds of notations appear on your script, they help you remember to reflect this information when you actually do the read.

Once my students have established that they understand the play and scene, their characters' purpose in making the story work, and what they specifically need in the scene from their partner, I allow them to read through the scene. If they violate the five-minute rule by a lot, I might stop them before they have completed their read, particularly if there are an enormous number of problems that must be dealt with in the first couple of minutes. I might also stop the scene if, in spite of passing the hot-seat questions, their choices as they actually read totally ignore or violate what they have established in the prior discussion. I also might stop the scene if one or both scene partners are simply reading their lines, oblivious to the fact that they are supposed to be listening and reacting to each other. Otherwise, I will allow the cutting to be read in its entirety.

After that awkward moment at the finish, when my student actors either look out toward me with those deer-in-the-headlight eyes or bow their heads and stop breathing, I will make some general comments about the scene. I always try to start with a bit of overall praise—unless the lack of scene preparation makes a positive comment unwarranted. I begin by listing in a general sense what worked in the scene and what did not. That is what you should expect from your own teacher. A good teacher will tell you what you did well and why, but mostly he or she should be talking to you about what you failed to accomplish and why. The reason for this emphasis is simple. There is little to be learned from what you did right. You already know that. What you want to hear is what you did wrong and why it did not work. That is where the learning comes in.

The subjects I might cover in my general comments include eye contact with the scene partner; listening and reacting to what is said and done in the scene, particularly with regard to new information, discoveries, victories, defeats, and other transitional moments; playing objectives fully and effectively; reading lines in a way that reflects what the other actor has just said or done; and clear progression of the unfolding scene. These are the basic issues that will affect the success of most work put up initially, and it is important that your teacher establish a pattern of how to address the issues of a scene. A patterned repetition will let you pick up that pattern more easily. It will help you develop your own craft so that you have a reliable set of points to work on as you initiate your independent work with a partner.

Comments should focus on what worked, what did not, and why. You don't need to hear teachers dwell on what they would have liked to have seen, or about how you should have done it. This kind of commentary falls into the category of directing and will not teach you how to work independently. Remember, your purpose in scene study is to develop the skills to make and carry out good choices, not just to execute the good choices someone else comes up with.

After your teacher gives big-picture comments, you will want to hear more specific notes. These notes should include moment-to-moment criticism, notes about what is not happening in the scene and should be, and things that need to played up or down and that will help you make the scene's story and your character's story stronger, clearer, and more compelling. I strongly advise you to take notes on what is being offered. Otherwise, by the time you rehearse again, you will not remember accurately what you are being asked to change, adjust, or add.

It is essential that your teacher, even if it means cutting off discussion time, allows you an opportunity to rework some of the scene. This should be a stop-and-go process, so that you can build improvements into your work with repetition and immediate feedback. The places in the scene you work should be the most troublesome parts of the scene, and/or parts that affect and influence the overall successful flow of the scene. Don't feel the need to work from beginning to end. First of all, there isn't enough time. Second of all, if you work episodically, you will begin to think about the structure of a scene in terms of what is happening in a beat, or even in a moment, and your ability to improve and adjust through craft rather than divine inspiration. Working individual beats will also help you visualize the sequential blocks of a scene that build one on top of the other. This kind of approach in class will reinforce the concept of working in rehearsal in the same manner. Your natural inclination when rehearsing will probably be to run the scene from beginning to end without stopping—which, of course, minimizes the opportunity to stop and create those inspired, individual moments that make the best acting so wonderful to watch.

In the previous section, I have focused on what you should expect from a teacher. I realize that if you happen to be a high school student or studying in a small college, you may not have an option to change teachers if your particular teacher does not fit the profile I have described. If that is the case, tuck the information away and look for that kind of teaching when the chance affords itself later on. In the meantime, try to think in terms of building your craft through finding answers rather than simply executing the solutions your teacher supplies. There are always ways of building on what has been offered. There are always problems that can be solved independently if you teach yourself to think in that way. If you do have the option of shopping for an acting teacher, try to find one who teaches rather than directs, one who is about making you smart rather than making you think he or she is.

Now, before closing our discussion on the first read, a few notes on some big-issue items that are worthy of attention.

Eye contact is extremely important. Reading the lines in real time in the first read is not essential, but listening is. You need to learn how to look at your script briefly, read a line or two to yourself, and then look up at your partner and deliver those lines while maintaining eye contact. Your partner should be looking at you and listening very carefully as you deliver your lines. Your partner is responsible not only for hearing your words, but for hearing what those words literally mean, both in the context of the scene and subtextually, if the script or actor's interpretation suggests that a subtextual meaning is communicated. (Some suggested exercises in the chapter called "Listening and Staying in the Moment" can help you learn to develop this difficult skill.)

Only when you have completed your delivery and your partner has reacted should she return to the script to find her next line. Then the process is repeated with you as the listener, and so on. When you and your partner adhere to this technique, you both can be sure that a connection will form between you and an ongoing thread will pull you both from moment to moment. Further, if this connection actually exists, listening and reacting will come from a real place—which is easier to act, by the way, than generating a bunch of manufactured reactions. Listening onstage that approximates the level of listening that most of us can maintain in life—that is, listening with all the senses—will help your recognize where the important moments are in a scene. Victories, defeats, new information, and discoveries are all worthy of response onstage, and actors who avail themselves of these opportunities are likely to make the most clear, believable, and interesting choices. When you focus only on your scripts, this essential element of the acting process cannot and will not occur.

One of the biggest errors my beginning scene study actors make is in regard to playing *objectives*. In spite of the big deal I make of playing objectives fully and specifically, my beginning actors seldom do it. When in the hot seat, my actors know that they will be grilled if they cannot articulate what they need from their scene partners, but once they get past that hurdle and are into the read, more often than not, they forget to go after their objectives. The fact is that acting is not like life, it just looks like it (in a realistic scene) when done well. In life, we seldom focus on a single objective and pursue it with all our heart all the time. But onstage, that is what you must learn to do. If you actually pursue your objectives at all times, the script will provide you and the audience with the variety and complexity of the character that is necessary, even though your choices may seem much more simplistic. The magic is that by playing and focusing on your objective, the scene is much more likely to be clear and effective than when you are trying to focus on character or emotion. It is vitally important that you train yourself to recognize this fact and develop your ability to play objectives effectively.

Many actors function under the illusion that a playwright's words pour spontaneously out of the mouth of the good actor, inflected perfectly to convey character and purpose. In a realistic scene, if you are truly listening to your scene partner, this can happen, but even among the best actors there is no guarantee. You must accept the fact that the playwright has provided the words of a script specifically and with great care to help make the story work a moment at a time. It is your job to discover the specific reasons for the word choice and the way the sentences are structured. You must combine the word usage with the objectives that you are playing. This process often requires analysis as well as listening in the moment. If you start to pay attention to the words that best convey your purpose (the operatives) from moment to moment in a scene, you will be much more likely to deliver a line with the ring of truth and with the dramatic punch that the playwright intended. Hitting the right words will also help you play your objective.

The most important thing you should come away with from the first read is a clear idea of what is going on in the scene and how your character contributes to the story—overall and a moment at a time. If you analyzed the scene effectively beforehand and made preliminary choices that are logical and effective, you will be able to spend much of your class time deepening moments and finding additional character choices that will help you as you begin blocking in the next round. You will also have more time to spend on listening and reacting in the moment. Finally, you will have more time to focus on playing your objectives specifically and on finding new and interesting ways of getting those objectives fulfilled through your use of the *tactics* you discover as you work through the scene with your teacher.

CHAPTER ELEVEN

BLOCKING— BEFORE THE SCENE IS PUT UP

I OFTEN HEAR MY STUDENTS TALKING ABOUT THE YOUNG actors they see on television, especially the ones that appear on shows like *Gossip Girls* or other teen-centered dramas. To call their commentary "harsh" would be an understatement. It would not be unfair to say that they are often unmercifully mean. What my students complain about most is the flatline delivery of the dialogue they hear. "Bad acting! Can't say their lines." This amuses me, because these same critical students are often the ones who in class are totally unable to make me believe a thing they do onstage physically. I don't believe their movements, and I find their bodies to be total enemies to whatever they are trying to accomplish on the stage. Yet I never hear my students complain about the young television actors' ability to walk, hug, kiss, and handle the props they work with. The fact is these television actors can do these things, and do them with such naturalness that we don't even think about them. More often than not, until I begin to harp on the physical aspect of their acting, my own students have not given an iota of thought to this part of their process.

Primarily, there are only two ways an audience can tell what you as a character are thinking and feeling: through what you say and how you say it, and through what you do and how you do it. The playwright gives you what you say, but what you do onstage, for the most part, is totally up to you. Many young actors have it in their heads that the director, like the champion on the white horse, will swoop in and magically give them all they need to do to make their brilliance emerge. An actor with that attitude is a lot like a firefighter who tries to take a taxi to the fire. He might do a great job once he gets there, but the cab has to show up first. It would be far more reliable for actors to accept the fact that they are responsible for making the story clear and compelling. It is ultimately the integration of what they do and say with how they do it and say it that allows the audience to read what they are thinking and feeling as a character.

It is not unusual for actors in roles with little or no dialogue to be highly praised for their work—Patty Duke or Melissa Gilbert as Helen Keller, for instance, or the remarkable silent performance of Robert Duval as Boo Radley in his movie debut in the classic *To Kill a Mockingbird*. When there is no dialogue, the audience becomes acutely aware of how much that actor communicates through other means. But good actors are always transmitting information through what they do and how they do it; it simply goes more unnoticed when they also have dialogue to work with. If you need a visual to know what I'm talking about, watch a bit of the brilliant Anthony Hopkins as the taciturn butler in *The Remains of the Day* or as Bernardo, the quiet assistant to Antonio Banderas in *Zorro.* If you need a bigger mallet to get the point, watch Hopkins steal the classic *The Silence of the Lambs* as Hannibal Lecter. What he chooses to do and not do physically is every bit as scary as what he says. He steals the film and is actually onscreen a very small part the time.

In the last several years I have noticed a trend in freshman students coming into my program, and I see the same thing on the audition tour each February. Increasingly, young actors act from their neck up. They don't know what to do with the rest of their bodies. This is a tremendous problem that, as an acting teacher, I spend more and more time addressing. The fact is, your acting skills need to extend below the neck—whether you're planning to act for the stage or for film.

BLOCKING BASICS

During the first read, you needed to demonstrate your understanding of the story of the scene, including the conflict, your objectives, your throughline of action or arc, and the big dramatic moments, which include all victories, defeats, new information, and discoveries. You also needed to demonstrate your ability to listen and react moment by moment and were offered criticism and suggestions for improvement. In addition, you were sent off knowing that for the second presentation of the scene, you would need to be up on your feet, moving through the set, and using what is on that set to create a reality for your characters. All of this must be done effectively if you are to be able to tell the story as compellingly and as believably as possible.

During your blocking rehearsals, you will have to work, for the most part, with three blocking components:

- Movement—when you must go from one place to another, and where you go once you choose to do so
- Business—any ongoing activity you engage in during the scene
- Gesture—any specific thing you do physically to get what you need.

This seems simple enough. However, when combined with dialogue and the need to make clear your character's thoughts, feelings, and driving needs, the choices available can seem almost infinite. As a result, some actors choose to ignore the need to deal with the blocking aspect of their acting obligation in any kind of specific manner. Many beginning actors seem to sense the need to be doing something but just can't put their finger on what they should be doing until it is too late to do it. Too often, moments come and go, leaving nothing in their wake but an awkward hesitation onstage, or worse, a series of moments that scream out with their emptiness or lack of clarity. For the reasons I listed at the top of this chapter, it is vital that you develop your physical skills. They are every bit as important as your ability to deliver a line of dialogue.

BEFORE THE REHEARSING BEGINS

Before you set off to begin your blocking rehearsals, it is essential that you understand that what you create or fail to create with regard to your set and use of props can make the difference between a scene that works and one that does not. Characters in realistic plays are seldom there just to talk. Most of the time characters are engaged in ongoing activity suggested by or directly provided in the script. Kitchens, for instance, often require particular kinds of activity and have items in them that can and should be used. In addition, the space in the kitchen, or in any other setting, can and should be used only in a purposeful manner. *Characters should move through space only when they need to do something or get something, or when they need to pursue someone or get away from someone.* Blocking becomes easier when seen with this kind of simplicity. All movement choices should be made with these purposes in mind, and just as with dialogue, you must choose to do things only if those things you choose to do serve your objective and are clear and believable when executed.

The set you come up with should reflect actual given circumstances implied or stated directly in the script. The more realistic the scene, the more specific and filled the actual set you design should be. In other words, in realistic plays, characters find themselves having dialogue with other characters while engaged in real activities. If your set design does not offer the possibility of engaging in real behavior while you speak, then you and your partner will find yourselves in the middle of an empty space, facing each other and delivering dialogue in a manner seldom engaged in during a real-life conversation.

In any Chekhov play, for example, characters engage in conversation that more often than not jumps from the banal, to the philosophical, to the emotionally heart-wrenching, almost imperceptibly. If the characters in a Chekhov play were standing in an empty space, these changes would be almost impossible to pull off. However, when characters can hide behind their ordinary day-to-day activities and obligations, these changes in conversational direction can be integrated into the action seamlessly and help make the actors playing these scenes come to life—because the real behavior that the sets and props afford them allows them to do so.

Here are two examples. In *Three Sisters,* Vershinin and Masha are having a conversation, one in which the Colonel is trying to make Masha understand how he really feels about her. The dialogue seems cliché-ridden and boring when the actors don't address the physical circumstances of the room they are in and what surrounds them in adjoining rooms. In actuality, it is their first intimate conversation, and there are guests in a nearby room threatening the couple's desire to be alone. As Vershinin advances on Masha, she uses the set to keep him at bay, fearing that if she does not keep her distance, the two of them will be discovered and compromised. The two of them are married—but not to each other. The setting of the scene and what surrounds the setting help provide the conflict as well as obstacles for this scene. Without a properly thought-out space, the scene cannot work.

In *Uncle Vanya,* an intimate conversation between Sonya and Yelena about their love, Astrov, is next to impossible to pull off—unless the set and props are being fully integrated and utilized by the actors playing the scene. It is amazing what activities like eating or clearing a table can do to turn a seemingly undeliverable line into the cap-off to a wonderful moment created through physical action. In the case of Yelena and Sonya, the arc of their developing intimacy, mutual admiration, and love is extremely difficult to make believable without such blocking. Their ongoing business is an integral part of the scene.

A NOTE ON MEMORIZATION

Today's acting student is not necessarily a good memorizer. Committing words and ideas to memory is no longer an educational concept held in high regard in many parts, and this lack of practice as part of your overall education may cause preparation problems for you. Memorizing lines may not be the most glamorous aspect of the acting process, but it is a necessary one. Proper preparation for a scene includes knowing your lines perfectly. I expect my students to have their lines down for the first put-up with blocking. I am not trying to be a hardass here. I hold this expectation for very practical reasons. If you don't have your lines down by the time you present your blocking scene, it will be extremely difficult for you to pull the scene off with any kind of effectiveness. How can you successfully look at and listen to your partner, handle props, and move through the scene if your script is still in front of your face? How can you create moments and react to them in sequences if you are constantly interrupting yourself by calling for lines? The answer is you cannot.

If you are slower than someone else with canning your lines, you may feel unfairly pressured, but I don't buy into this argument. All of us have strengths and weakness that we use to our advantage or must overcome by working harder. So it is with memorization. If you want to become an actor, then part of your burden will be to get those lines down just like the fast memorizers do. No director will want to be wasting his or her time and money accommodating actors who are unable to meet their basic responsibilities.

BEFORE PUTTING UP THE SCENE

Before you put up your scene, it is always a good idea to point out and describe to the class the set you have designed for your work. If your studio or classroom is like mine, the physical layout of the scene needs to be explained—because much of it will not actually be present. Walls, windows, doors, and other structural elements may be implied through your actions but may not be delineated specifically enough for the audience to make a mental picture, especially the first time the scene is put up. Therefore, it is a good idea that you lay out for your audience what they should be seeing. Your purpose here is to choose and explain only those elements that must be explained so that there is no distraction to the effectiveness of your work.

You might also want to explain what props you will actually be using in the scene, and what props you may be simulating because they are not physically present. A note here about consistency and the world of the play, however. An audience can be made to believe anything they see onstage—if the choices made have a consistency and logic that is maintained in the universe of the play. It may be an artistic choice to use no props in a scene, or it may be a practical one. But when choices are not clear and consistent, that lack of an established convention can become distracting to an audience.

Let me be more specific with an example. Suppose you decide to use eating utensils during your scene that takes place at the dinner table. It is a scene from *The Dining Room,* and the characters are upscale New Englanders—the kind that A. R. Gurney writes about so well. You have made the choice to use utensils because you can easily lift some knives and forks from the cafeteria. You also bring in paper plates from home because paper plates are no problem to fit into your backpacks. However, you could not find any wine or water glasses also needed for the scene and have decided to mime the drinking aspects of your stage business. So what exactly are you presenting here? Upscale characters eating imaginary food on paper plates with real knives and forks, drinking from invisible wine and water glasses. If one of the characteristics of good acting is believability, then you have inadvertently made it harder on yourself to succeed.

Especially at the beginning of their study with me, many of my actors fail to bring props with them to class. Often they will ask me right before it is time for them to put up their scene whether I have this prop or that. If I tell them

I don't have a particular prop, they decide they will simulate the prop during the scene. This situation raises several issues. Did they rehearse their scene at home without props? If so, did they make choices about their use during the scene? Did they work out when they will lift the water glass or the wine glass and why are they lifting it at this particular moment? Is it a matter of thirst, discomfort, or something else? When did they decide to actually drink once the glass *is* lifted? Before, after, or during a line they deliver? Before, after, or during a line that the scene partner delivers? How much will they drink when they drink? What effect, if any, does the amount of drinking have on the other character? What judgments about drinking is the audience supposed to be making? When does the glass get put down?

All of these questions and many, many more are worthy of your consideration. The answers to questions like these can help you define the movement and business choices you make, because they will contribute to the story you are trying to tell. These physical actions may not be mentioned in the script, but they are certainly implied by the very fact that the author makes the scene occur during a meal. If you rehearse your scene without actually using glasses, chances are that most of the questions raised above will probably never even occur to you. If the props are not actually there, you will focus only on the dialogue and yourself and will miss an enormous number of opportunities to tell the story of the scene in a practical and realistic way.

Now let's go the other way for a moment. Suppose I have the props requested, and I give my actors a set of water and wine glasses. In all probability, these actors will gratefully take the props and simply wing their use, sometimes to surprising, but seldom to helpful, ends during their presentation. The unfamiliarity of the glasses might make the actors look and feel awkward during their scene, distracting them or the watching audience. If they chose to fill the glasses, they might be dealing with the liquid for the first time, no problem in life, but a significant problem for unrehearsed, nervous actors. Can they coordinate their drinking with their other obligations in the moment? Can they lift and lower their glasses without spilling? Can they time out their drinking to make effective moments? Will they find it necessary to gesture while their glass is still in hand, and what will the results of that be? Or will they, as is often the case, gratefully thank me for the glasses and then find no opportunities for their use during the course of the scene? Truly, any of these possibilities is a good bet.

115

The moral, then, is this. You should think about the props you will need and rehearse with them in a very specific way. Ultimately, the use of props should not be random. They can and will help you communicate the story of the scene, as well as the story of your individual character. They will also ground your work in a reality that miming is unlikely to provide. But this will happen only if you are willing to think about how to effectively use your props to tell the story and if you are observant to the spontaneous and useful accidental moments that occur during your rehearsals.

Here is an example of the fortunate "in the moment" accident. Suppose actor A spontaneously downs a big slug of wine after announcing that his brother is gay, inadvertently making a statement about what he thinks of his brother's sexual persuasion and, because of the choice, about his own character. The actor may not have planned this moment, but it certainly was an effective accident. The actors rehearsing might want to appropriate this piece of serendipitous action into their scene permanently. This is how actors must learn to work. If the glass were not present, if the glass were not filled with liquid, this acting moment would, in all likelihood, never be discovered. We must be willing to work in this fashion.

On the other hand, many of the things you do with props can help tell the audience what you are thinking and feeling in a moment. Consider this fact from the outset. You should, during your rehearsal process, actively think about how and when your specific use of props and movement can help tell your story. When you drink, and/or how you drink, can help define a moment or make clear your arc through the story of the scene. Ongoing business that stops, for instance—you put down the newspaper to make momentary eye contact, you go suddenly to the bar and pour another drink with an intensity you didn't have a moment before, you stop drying the dish you have been focused on—can tell the story of what you are thinking and feeling, even when you are thinking and feeling nothing. This is smart acting. This is craft that you can rely on even when you are not on your best game.

Once you have taken your audience through the elements of the set and the props you will use, explain what the audience will need to know in order to understand the scene. Any relevant given circumstances brought out in earlier scenes, but not explained in the scene itself, should be included. It might also be a good idea to explain how your choices for the set reflect necessary circumstances of the scene and play, and how they contribute to the story you are about to tell. Be sure to relate only given circumstances that need to be understood in order to make the scene work. You should not be telling the story of the scene itself. If you have done your work properly, that will be made clear as the scene unfolds.

MORE ON BLOCKING AND WORKING THE SCENE

REMEMBER, YOUR PURPOSE IN A SCENE STUDY CLASS is to develop your ability to work independently—to be able to analyze and execute choices that work. It is not enough to see your scene from your character's point of view or from the viewpoint of the playwright. You must also learn to envision your scene from the viewpoint of the audience. It is important for you to be able to step back from the scene and see it as the audience does. Ask yourself what they must be able to see in terms of the action of the scene and in terms of the characters' interaction, thoughts, and feelings. Your job is to get all of that information across to the audience. The clarity and imaginative use of your physical action in the scene is essential for doing this successfully. That again is why you don't want your teacher to be supplying you with solutions. But whether your teacher provides you with solutions or not, you want to learn to think on your own; keep asking yourself what the audience should be seeing and hearing in order for the story arc to make sense and be compelling.

As we all know, acting is often defined as behaving believably in fictional circumstances. Most of us are capable of doing this to some degree. But keep in mind the three-pronged definition of good acting that has been cited throughout this book: to be believable and tell the best possible story while serving the script. This definition suggests that, yes, actors must be believable onstage, but in addition, they have a responsibility to make the most interesting choices they can, by bringing out the best in the script, not by working against it or by being self-serving. Choices that may make an actor seem impressive to an audience, but work at the expense of the intent of the script, are simply not good choices.

I always tell my students that I will comment on their work from the viewpoint of an intelligent alien creature. In other words, I will see and hear only what the actors specifically communicate, not what I think they are trying to communicate. This is an important distinction. I often brag that I intend to be the dumbest member of the audience and that I am not interested in deciphering what is going on through implication. I will not do more thinking than a paying audience would. You need to learn how to make choices that communicate in just that way. An audience should not have to interpret your choices. You should make your character's thoughts and feelings clear—unless the script mandates vagueness for plot purposes.

Students have a tendency to be very generous when commenting on the work of their peers. You probably are, too. Unconsciously, you empathize with the actors who are performing and often accept and claim to like work that you would never rate so highly if you were watching actors you were unfamiliar with or that you are paying a lot of money to see. I call this the "sympathy factor." I believe this phenomenon occurs because without trying to, student actors realize they, too, will be in the same boat very soon, and they choose to be generous in the hopes that they will be treated with kindness when it is their turn to perform. Good teachers will not fall into this trap. Their job, when you perform your scenes, is to report accurately and clearly on what they see and hear, on what they understand and what they don't, on what works and what doesn't work—all from the point of view of the audience. If this is the way your teacher operates, it is his or her comments that you should be paying attention to, not those of your peers. If there is contradiction, do what your teacher suggests. Your teacher is the professional.

You should always take notes on what your teacher says, by the way. If you do not write them down, you will forget them by the time you rehearse the scene again, or worse, you will remember how the notes made you feel rather than their specific, objective contents. Nothing is more frustrating than bringing in a revised scene that repeats the errors of the previous work or that has gone completely in the wrong direction because of a misunderstanding that resulted from bad memory or faulty notes.

I suggest that when taking notes, you arrange them starting with the big picture rather than details. You might want to think in terms of the following categories:

- Clarity
- Story progression
- Believability
- Stakes

First determine what parts of the story you told were clear and what parts were not. If the lack of clarity resulted from certain blocking choices, you will want to rethink them. You will also want to think about what moments you emphasized if the arc of the story was not clear. If you got notes on believability, you will have to address that, as well. Often your believability depends on listening and reacting. If you were failing to do those things, you will need to work on that aspect of your process. Finally, even if you were doing all of the above, you may have gotten notes regarding the fact that your choices were not interesting enough, or as interesting as they could or should have been. If your work is not interesting, that is usually a result of your failure to make the stakes in the scene as high as they needed to be. You will need to make appropriate adjustments.

Let's take a look at some examples to make clear what I'm talking about—the movement and business of the scene, for instance. You must learn how to tell the story of the scene through what you do physically, as well as through your positioning relative to another actor. In spite of what you may have thought, this physical acting is part of your craft. It will help make you clear, interesting, and believable onstage. You must also learn to use movement to make clear your objectives and changing relationship with fellow characters. Here's an example from an often-used scene from *The Glass Menagerie.*

Jim, the gentleman caller, enters the living room with a candelabra shortly after the lights have gone out. He sees Laura sitting on the couch. The actors have staged their scene so that as it opens, Jim immediately enters and crosses toward Laura while he says his opening lines. While he is standing close to Laura, the two begin to engage in conversation. This is the kind of blocking you might come up with, particularly in the first weeks of a scene study class. What is wrong with this picture?

In the first place, Laura has an opportunity to establish, through her business, how she is feeling. Perhaps the actor playing Laura has chosen to use the glass menagerie but has not had time to develop anything before Jim's entrance. Playing with her glass animals is potentially an excellent choice. The fact that she plays with her little animals, and how she does so, can be both interesting and revealing—if the audience is given the opportunity to witness it. Remember, you need to develop your ability to communicate through your use of physical action. If Laura is playing with her menagerie, and Jim sees her doing so, an interesting moment can be made on his entrance. This moment should not be diluted or destroyed by his crossing too soon without registering somehow what he has seen. Narrowing the space between Laura and himself is one of Jim's objectives. But if the actor playing Jim eliminates that distance immediately, he kills the opportunity of telling the story of how he cleverly gets Laura to accept some physical intimacy. Therefore, using blocking effectively is essential here. Finally, Jim and Laura being in close proximity, having a conversation for a long stretch of time, suggests a kind of comfort between them that probably should not exist until it is earned, and the story of that earning is too interesting to throw away. Look at all there is to talk about just in the opening moments of the scene. This is the kind of physical sequence you can work on—once your teacher has reacted and given notes on your work.

Now here's an example of using blocking to make the story progression work. The story just described is about how Jim, through his social abilities, overcomes Laura's resistance and, by the end of the lovely scene, actually has her thinking there is a possibility of an ongoing relationship between them. Because of Laura's debilitating shyness, the journey is actually enormous and makes for a fascinating and heartbreaking scene. Physically, the scene is about breaking through the wall of psychological distance and creating intimacy. The question you will have to answer in a scene like this is, how can you do this physically to tell the story to the audience? When phrased this way, the answer becomes almost obvious. The space between Jim and Laura can tell the story. It is Jim's job to minimize the physical distance, Laura's to maintain it—until she chooses to allow that distance to be reduced and, eventually, eliminated. If you learn to see the scene in these terms, your blocking choices will quickly become easier to find and execute.

More than anything else, what makes the story of this scene believable or not are Laura's moment-to-moment reactions as Jim tries to get through her resistance. For each of his attempts at narrowing the distance between them, Laura must have an answer or reaction. Most of the time her response is not in the lines she is given—because Jim's objective is played as much through what he does as through what he says. The audience must see Laura's reactions to Jim's every attempt to narrow the physical distance between them. The actors in the scene must play off of each other at every moment. When they do, the story becomes clear, exciting, and, of course, believable. You must first learn to see this physical aspect of storytelling, and then find a way to make it happen onstage.

Finally, what are the stakes in this little scene? It is not just a story about allowing a boy to know that you like him. It is a story about one last chance to find someone to save you from a life of desperation. It is a story about thinking, just when you have completely given up on life, that your deepest wish is to be fulfilled, and then having that dream dashed at the very moment you think it may come true. The actor portraying Laura must play the scene in the manner I have just described. For Jim, the scene is a story of rediscovering the power he has over other people, the power he had in high school, but seems to have lost in the world of grown-up problems and pressures. His need for success here is almost a desperate one, and his moment-by-moment victories in the scene are pulling him from the fire of defeat. You must learn to see the scene in this manner and then learn to play it through physical choices that make the stakes clear.

Once your teacher gives you notes on your scene, there may be time to work it in class with his or her help. If your class is like mine, there will not be an enormous amount of time to do so. You may not have the time to work the scene from beginning to end. What your teacher will probably do if that is the case is to select certain parts of the scene to work on. These will probably be the parts of the scene that have given you and your partner the most trouble, or sections that must be made to work if what follows is to work. Don't be bothered if your teacher jumps around. It will help you understand that a scene is indeed composed of a series of blocks that can be seen as independent little stories that fit together, almost like a set of Legos. When these pieces are properly placed, the entire structure is both beautiful and solid.

I will often make my students repeat moments and beats several times, until they make a section work or until they recognize its potential for working. Once you understand what is going on in a moment or beat, you will be able to go off and rehearse it until you get it on your own. After your session is over, be sure you write down anything you have learned from the workthrough, and be sure to use it or build on it when you work on the scene again.

FURTHER WORKTHROUGHS

In each subsequent put-up of the scene, you should first address any issues brought up and/or worked on in the previous put-up. Each of these issues should be fixed and/or added to in your rehearsal process to the best of your ability. By added to, I mean that changing something may lead to further ideas or more changes that are consistent with the new forward progression of the scene. If the scene has been properly rehearsed using the notes from the previous presentation, you should find that your scene is much improved. However, it is not unusual for a whole new set of problems to be created when you address the old ones. As the scene goes in a new direction, new dynamics will replace the old, and new problems inevitably appear. This may upset you at first, but if you realize that this is all part of the process, the new notes you get can be considered your latest gift package for growth.

It is also possible that you will get notes that seem to contradict things you might have been told in the previous presentation. This, too, is not an unusual occurrence. Any changes the scene has undergone since the last time can alter the relationship between one moment and the next, between the characters playing those moments, and even between what works and what doesn't. Remember that since there is no director, your scene is continuing to evolve without a pilot steering the boat on one specific course. New ideas will continue to alter the map, and new directions will need to be taken to find your way home. Consider the process to be similar to tacking a sailboat. You'll simply have to zig and zag your way to your destination.

If you spend too much time evaluating the worth of your teacher's notes and suggestions, rather than giving your notes a try, there is probably a problem—a problem not unusual in the early goings of a scene study class. Either you find it difficult to hear criticism, or your teacher is not a good one. If the latter, change your teacher if and when possible. If the former, you will need to learn to treat criticism as a gift. From praise you will learn very little that is useful. But by taking criticism and finding ways to improve your work, you are learning to master your craft. And that's your purpose for taking the class, right?

In the first put-ups of your scene, you should be focusing on the basics—blocking, objectives, listening, and so on. But as your understanding of the scene develops and you become more sophisticated about the work, you should begin to focus on its subtler aspects. Not only should moments continue to be more clearly defined and deepened, but character development should be progressing, as well. I spend very little time talking about "character" per se, particularly in a beginning scene study class. I believe that 70 percent of character is action. What the actor chooses to do as a character, and the manner in which those choices are carried out, goes a long way toward creating character for an audience. When young actors think in terms of "their character" rather than the obligations of the scene, it can be a dangerous thing.

However, as the scene progresses, you should be thinking more about the externals of your characters, because these externals can and do help tell the story of the scene. How your character talks and walks and dresses can all be important aspects in helping bring your character, as well as the story of the scene, to life. Finding the rhythm, tempo, and energy sources of your character will make the work more specific, clear, and interesting, and therefore, your work will be more effective. Once the basics of the scene are being communicated to the audience, you should be developing these external aspects of the work.

For instance, once a scene is on its feet, you should wear costume items suggestive of your character. Dressing appropriately can help you find the physicality of the role you are playing. Looking at it from another angle, sneakers won't help an actor feel like a late nineteenth-century Norwegian scholar, and a halter top and navel ring probably won't help an actress find the soul of his unhappy and constricted wife, Hedda. Sneakers and halter tops are in no way physically appropriate for the time, place, and character of the world of the play. Actors serious about their craft will choose to work in clothing that will help them find and simulate this world, not distract them from it. You must learn to think in this way.

Vocal choices and dialects can help define character, as well, and you should explore this physicality when appropriate to do so, but not before the basics have been found and established. A scene is not about the accent, and young actors who throw in the accent before understanding more important scene dynamics will sometimes get stuck in the voice rather than pursue a character's action. There is nothing harder to break out of than a Tennessee

Williams scene in which the actors all sound like Foghorn Leghorn and seem to be saying dialogue for no other reason than to sound southern. On the other hand, a regional dialect often helps the actor find the rhythms of speech and character points in a play written clearly with a particular dialect in mind. Ultimately, it is up to you to take on the requirements of the scene according to a specific set of priorities. Keep in mind that an artist sketches first, establishes the composition, and then paints in the detail and color. Hopefully, this is a useful metaphor for how you ultimately paint the picture of the scenes you will work on.

A FINAL NOTE

How many times you should put up a particular scene can be a subject of debate. The mastery of a scene is a process that you must pursue intently. At the same time, a product is not your ultimate goal here. What you want is to develop the skills necessary to successfully work independently. Enthusiasm and commitment are essential if you are to reach that goal. When you discover that your enthusiasm is ebbing—because you have lost interest in a particular scene—then you should move on, even if you have not completely solved the problems a particular scene has offered up. Any lessons left unlearned from the experience of one scene will no doubt be revisited while working on another. If you keep that in mind, you should be able to find the necessary balance between process and product. You must never allow yourself to settle for less than your best effort when developing your craft. If you can permanently plant this attitude in your heart and mind, you can rest easy, knowing that excellence is something you will strive for and ultimately achieve.

CHAPTER
THIRTEEN

LISTENING AND STAYING IN THE MOMENT

DURING THE COURSE OF YOUR EDUCATION YOU'VE probably heard your teachers say countless times, "I just told you that! You're not listening!" Often this is said in the context of someone asking a question she answered just a moment before, or an assignment given the previous day that only three people out of thirty seemed to have heard. The truth is we have become a society of bad listeners. Many theories attempt to explain this phenomenon, everything from the argument that we have become a visual society—television replaced radio, remember—to the hypothesis that we have become a selfish society more interested in hearing ourselves talk than listening to others. The fact is, whatever the reasons, listening is something we do not do very well as a culture. Yet this skill is absolutely necessary to any actor.

In life, it's when things are hanging in the balance, when our well-being depends upon it, that we really start to listen. This is true even for those of us who are bad listeners. When your father starts to tell you why you won't be using the car for the next month, you're probably listening. When your girlfriend starts explaining why she's through with you, you're probably listening. When the cop pulls you over at five till midnight and asks you for your license, better believe you're listening. And while you're listening in these fraught situations, you're probably listening with all your senses. You're taking in everything with your ears, your eyes—even through your skin. You're looking for road out, a scheme to save yourself, a way to turn this awful event around, a way to draw victory from defeat. These real-life examples are high-staked situations, ones that require your complete attention.

Those intense situations are the kinds of circumstances that plays and movie scripts are all about. What happens onstage or on film, though it resembles everyday life, is seldom like everyday day life for long. As you well know by now, plays and films must tell good stories if they are to succeed, and good stories require conflict and big stakes—plus the twists and turns that guarantee the audience will want to see what happens next.

The last several chapters have discussed this dynamic in detail. Conflict, the engine of drama, you'll remember, is the playwright's best friend. It is also the actors'. A good actor must find the conflict in the acting situation, determine the objectives to be played, and find the physical actions to carry out these objectives. This is all part of the homework and rehearsal process that any good actor goes through. As actors we must learn to make choices that tell the story clearly and compellingly while being consistent with the demands of the script. In other words, we must take what the playwright has given us through the script and not only bring it to life, but, hopefully, enhance it. If we're good actors, we learn to make exciting choices and execute them clearly and smoothly so that they resemble what people do in life. When we're well rehearsed, we get our choices so into our bones and psyches that we no longer have to think about them, thus making them seem totally spontaneous.

But in spite of how well you rehearse and how well you know what you're supposed to do, nothing onstage ever happens quite the same way twice—because it's happening live. Actors don't always do exactly the same thing, and they don't always say what they have to say in exactly the same way. At least, good actors don't. Good actors continue to pursue their objectives at all times, of course, but they are sensitive to any and all atmospheric changes, to the nuances that pop up before them. That means that they will adjust according to what is going on in the moment just as they would in life. When two good actors work together, the give and take between them keeps things fresh, alive, and new. That, by the way, often marks the difference between the amateur performer, and those who act well on the college level and in the profession. The amateur is often praised for her energy and her ability to put it out there consistently no matter what is happening around her. But if this performer disregards or ignores what is happening around her, chances are, what she does will look less than real or believable. And she is liable to sound canned or hammy rather than spontaneous. If you play your choices exactly as you rehearsed them without regard for the nuances and subtle changes that may occur, you will look like you are *acting* rather than living in the moment. And if you fail to back-burner what you have rehearsed, and trust that it really is planted in your bones and psyches, you will not be available during your stage life to notice and react to the new stuff that is happening all the time. Any good actor will tell you that acting is reacting. You can't react to what you don't see and hear. And it's those reactions that keep actors vibrant and compelling, and audiences on the edges of their seats.

In the last couple of years, I have been doing what I used to think was a very simple game with my beginning acting students. The game goes something like this. I have my students sit in a large circle with their legs crossed. I tell them we will be playing a repetition game—one in which they will have to watch and listen carefully if they are to play effectively. I tell them that the game is simple. All they will have to do is repeat exactly what the person before them says and does. I then give the first person a phrase to repeat to the person sitting next to him or her. Since we are playing in a circle, I make an arbitrary decision where to start and tell that first person to repeat the message either to the person to her left or right. It doesn't matter. We will be changing directions repeatedly as the game goes on. The message I give to the first person might be something like this:

You can lead a horse to water, but you can't make him drink,

or

You can lead a horse to water, but you can't make him sink,

or

The early bird catches no moss or rolling stones.

I might offer up a quote from Shakespeare, read a safety direction on the wall that catches my eye, or simply make something up extemporaneously. It doesn't matter. The point is that all members of the class are to repeat exactly what they have seen and heard from the person before them, and they must repeat it exactly as they have seen and heard it, down to the smallest detail. Easy, right?

Before the game begins, I inform my students about the importance of listening as an actor. More specifically, I tell them that being able to listen onstage is as important as the most important tools they are taught during their acting studies. I also tell them that the term *listening* doesn't refer only to what the ears do. It means listening with all the senses—with the eyes, with touch, with everything, as they would in life. I tell them that in life we take in information about the people who surround us using *all* our senses.

Even in conversation, we learn as much from what people do as from what they say, and we learn as much from how people say what they say as from the words themselves. We watch body language, we listen for nuance, we put context onto the literal words being said. We look for subtext in the context. We constantly process the information we receive. We analyze even when we are not aware of it. We use our intuitive processes or our primitive fight-or-flight equipment as much as we use logic and reason. We react to stuff we are not even consciously aware of. This is what we do in life, and this must be part of what we do onstage—or what we do onstage will not be believable.

After that introduction, I give the first person the phrase or sentence she must repeat. I look her directly in the eyes and lean in close to her face as I say the line, "Water is life, my friend, no more, no less." Or something equally weird. Depending on what I say, the class will laugh or grow silent in response to the line, or in anticipation of the repetition. Everyone will be focused, attentive to the extreme. The person I am talking to will either laugh along with the class or will be so concentrated that she will ignore what surrounds her. She will take in my phrase, turn to the person to the left, and repeat what I just said—exactly as I delivered it, soundwise and physically.

Except it never happens this way.

The game almost never gets past the first or second person without me having to stop the action. My students can't seem to repeat what they've heard in the manner it is said to them. And they almost always ignore part of the intro speech I have just given them—the part about listening with all their senses. Either they change the reading of the line (a different word is emphasized), or they alter the music of the line (the actual musical pitches given to each of the words are changed), or they add or take away pauses. Often my actors don't even get the words right. (I know that's hard to believe, but it's true nonetheless.) Physically, eye contact changes, body gestures are missed or altered, or there is no give and take (the moment-to-moment discovery and reaction to what is being said—which in life we do automatically).

Once I do allow the game to go from person to person several times without interruption—in spite of the fact that the repetition has not been copied accurately—actors will miss major changes, as well, and will simply default back to an earlier version of what was said and done. I once had a student who, with a slip of the tongue, accidentally changed "The early bird catches the worm" to "The early bird catches the word," and the receiving person proceeded to go back to "worm" when he passed the sentence on. Everyone else caught the slip and laughed, but the receiver had been totally oblivious. This happens quite often, actually. So why is this? How can this be?

The short answer is we don't listen, especially when we're acting. Often the receivers in the game are so worried about getting it right—focusing on remembering what has been said and done up to that point, or busy cataloguing what they must do—that they are simply unavailable to do what the game is all about: simply listening and reacting to the person speaking to us. Most of us are guilty of this acting contradiction. I know I am. Here is a little confession. When I occasionally act, I find that especially in the early stages of rehearsal—the part where I'm still learning my lines—I sometimes don't recognize the cue lines when my partner says them. Often it is because I'm only half listening. I'm focused instead on what I need to say next. In other words, I'm busy thinking about my next line when I should be listening with all my senses to my partner. What I say next almost always comes directly from what I as the character have just heard. The playwright wrote it that way, after all. Obviously, if I'm not fully listening, coming up with my next line will be more difficult, since each line is inspired by the previous one.

On the other hand, when I'm teaching an acting class, if my actors are struggling with their lines, I can often feed them their next line—simply because I have heard them repeat it a couple of times. When I come up with the lines spontaneously, it usually surprises me, and it always impresses the class. They think I have every play in the world memorized. But the truth is, I was simply listening effectively. It's my job as a teacher to listen with all my senses to everything happening onstage, so I can respond effectively as a teacher. Listening with that kind of intensity is also the actor's job, but as actors our priorities are sometimes in the wrong place. When you're working with your partner, your priority needs to be on listening and reacting to him.

The previous chapters focused on analysis and synthesis—figuring out what's going on in the script and finding effective ways to do what is needed in order to make it all work. But ultimately, when you're onstage or when the cameras are rolling, if you're not listening, all the other work you have done will be for naught. Even the best choices, if delivered in such a way that the audience doesn't believe, can be diminished, if not destroyed. On the other hand, ironically, compelling moment-to-moment work can make an audience completely forget that what you are doing may have little to do with the forwarding the play the playwright has given you. My own definition of good acting—acting that is believable and tells the best possible story while serving the script—acknowledges the three overall obligations of the acting process. Of course it is the actor's obligation to effectively tell the story the playwright has provided, but believability will always have primacy. And believability is totally connected with your skill at listening.

If you've ever watched a prepared first reading of a scene in acting class, you know just what I'm talking about. By *prepared first reading* I mean that first time you put up a scene with a partner. You've done your homework—analyzed the scene, made choices about how you're going to tell the story. You've identified the conflict, isolated your objectives, and know where the big moments are. Although you haven't memorized the lines, you are familiar enough with them so that you can read without stumbling. If you're a student in my class, you do that first read sitting down, because I don't want you to have to worry about all your physicality right now. Too many balls to juggle for the first time up. So basically all you have to do is execute your choices in terms of objectives—and listen. Sounds simple enough, right? But what happens?

In the first several weeks of my intro to scene study class, even after repeated warnings and explanations about how the first read should be done, most of the time my actors keep their noses in their scripts the entire reading. If they do ever look at each other, the eye contacts are so brief, it's like giving the other actor an occasional kiss on the cheek and thinking you've made love. This, of course, prevents the actors from picking up on any of the in-the-moment things that might be going on and building on them—the most important way to add depth to the story provided by the playwright. And the main reason there is no eye contact? I suspect it's because the actors are afraid they won't be ready to say their next line. But by focusing entirely on what they will be saying next, they miss the opportunity to make an acting moment by listening and being in that moment. In another piece of irony, it is the finding and making of moments that make actors good actors—not being able to read the words from a script. Why, then, are so many young actors obsessed with reading the lines rather than playing the moments that tell the story?

My guess is that many young actors think the words of a script are synonymous with the story of the play. That the words are the be-alls and end-alls of acting. But they're not. Dialogue is just one of the tools a playwright uses to tell the story. There is also the action. But most of the action, physical and otherwise, is implied rather than stated directly by the playwright, or it must be figured out from scratch by actors and their directors. All this storytelling action is every bit as important as the words being said—just ask anyone who has ever acted in a Chekhov play. So moments should be discovered through homework, of course, but they also must be uncovered through listening and reacting. Every actor reads a play and makes a movie in his head picturing how the play should go. But no actor and his scene partner will ever have the identical movie. Therefore each of them must throw out their own version and find a new movie together, one that is built through listening to each other and through making the necessary adjustments.

That's why it drives me crazy that my actors insist on keeping their noses in the book. Every time I force my students to start looking at each other, they start listening, as well—with all their senses. Immediately, there is a connection that is more fun to watch, and that makes the story fuller and clearer. The actors start reacting to each other, and those reactions start becoming spontaneous—which in turn creates new colors to be used and reacted to, and also makes the arc of the storyline more interesting. The fact is in a first read, no one cares if you have to interrupt yourself and pause to find the next line. The payoff is always worth it.

With practice, any actor can learn to look down at his script, take in a line or two, look up, and deliver it effectively to his scene partner. You can teach yourself the discipline to keep eye contact until your scene partner completes his or her response to you. And you can train yourself to do all that before you return to your script, where the process will begin again. Whatever is lost by having to pause to find the next line will be made up a thousand times over by what is gained through the listening and reacting process.

Keep in mind that the kind of listening we're talking about here extends to your other senses, as well. What you learn from eye contact includes all the information you get from body language, and gesture and movement, too. Any in-the-moment physicality can produce a moment and a reaction as much as the words do. This idea also extends to props and scenery when you get to those things later in the rehearsal process.

You enter the room. You see a bottle on the table. Why is the vodka sitting out? The window shades are pulled, but it's the middle of the day. What's going on? There's music playing on the stereo. Hmm. Why is your scene partner sitting on the sofa in her underwear? Why are her legs crossed seductively? Why is she wearing those sunglasses? Why does she uncross her legs as you move toward her? This last item is a blocking choice, but even a first reading in my class can be filled with subtle in-the-chair physicalization that can and should be dealt with.

You say something, and your scene partner leans in toward you. What does that tell you? How does that change you? What adjustments should you make? Your scene partner leans away. What do you learn from that? What does it cause you to do? Your scene partner touches you. What does that mean? How do you react? How should you react? It certainly produces a moment that you might not have been aware of. When we are touched in life, it is often a big deal. Onstage we are always on the lookout for a big deal to play, and here is one that flies right into your glove. Squeeze it. Use it. You say your next line in response to the touch you've been given. Suddenly the line takes on a different meaning, something that is connected to that touch. That is far better than the old movie you gave up when you took on a partner. You lean in, you touch your scene partner back. She averts her eyes. What does that mean? You pull your hand away. Your scene partner looks back at you and smiles. She says her next line. It now means something completely different. You get the idea. Listening happens with all your senses.

If you ever have a chance to watch professional actors read for a role, you will notice that the ones who most impress you are the ones who are making eye contact. They are listening and reacting. They are finding moments and doing things. They are building on what they are receiving. Almost invariably, this is the kind of actor who ultimately gets the roles. I also know through my own experience as an actor that when I audition with someone who insists on staying connected with me, not only is the scene better, but I am better, too. Being forced to react brings out my truer, more compelling stuff. The director, in turn, gets far more excited when things are happening between actors than when someone is chewing the furniture all by himself. If there are two people onstage, there had better be stuff happening between them. That means listening, listening, listening.

So, in conclusion, as an actor, there are three primary things you'll need to learn how to do—if you're going to have the requisite tools for success. You'll need to be able to analyze a script, you'll need to be able to translate what you've learned from your analysis into actions that you can play clearly and compellingly on the stage, and you'll need to be able to integrate all of that so well into your body and mind that you will be able to live in the moment onstage. If you are going to be believable, you will simply have to be available to see what the audience is able to see and respond to everything that's there—just as you do in life. All of these skills take practice and dedication. Developing your skills as an actor is no different than developing the skills for playing the piano or for dancing. You must put in the time. Because acting looks so easy when it's well done, actors often forget that fact. It's the what-you-do-and-how-you-do-it part that takes all the time and work. It's the what-you-do-and-how-you-do-it part that ultimately makes you the artist. But artists work through their craft. And that's what must keep improving. So—keep practicing. And listening—at every moment.

SOME EXERCISES FOR FURTHER EXPLORATION

The legendary Sanford Meisner spent his career as an acting teacher focused on the listening elements of acting. The repetition games he invented are among the best ways to develop your onstage listening skills. Several books by or about Meisner and his work are available. Two of the most read are *Sanford Meisner on Acting*, by Sanford Meisner and Dennis Longwell, and *The Sanford Meisner Approach,* a series of books by Larry Silverberg. You might want to check some of these out.

For a few immediate quick fixes, however, try one or more of the following games. For best results, do these exercises while actually rehearsing a scene with your partner before you bring it into class:

1. After your partner delivers a line, simply say, "What?"

   This will give your partner a chance to say her line again, and it will give you another shot at listening specifically to what is being said to you. Her line will probably improve, because she will intensify it. Yours will improve because she has intensified it, and because you've now had a second chance to put your listening hat on.

2. Repeat each line from the script that your partner says to you. You may change the pronouns. For instance,

   Your partner says the line, "I never much liked you."
   You say, "You never much liked me."
   Your partner says, "You never gave me anything; you were a lousy brother."
   You say, "I never gave you anything; I was a lousy brother."
   This exercise guarantees that you've heard what was said to you and forces you to consider the context and subtext.

3. After you deliver a line, say, "What did I just say?"

   This will keep you connected with your partner and will challenge him into making sure that he is listening. Demanding his attention will probably result in his giving it to you. As a variation, try not asking the question after every line. Surprise him. That way you keep your partner on his toes and force him to listen on his own.

4. After your scene partner delivers a line, say, "What is that supposed to mean?"

   Your scene partner will then be forced to explain improvisationally her subtext and to actually know why she is saying what she says. It will remind you to listen specifically to what is being said—because as an actor you have to!

CHAPTER FOURTEEN

FINAL
NOTES

IF YOU'VE BEEN ACTING OR STUDYING THE CRAFT OF acting for more than a little while, you've probably read your fair share of articles and books on the subject, and you're probably aware that there are several approaches to the craft—early or late Stanislavki, Method, et cetera, et cetera. Each approach has its share of followers, some of whom may even be fanatics about the one they adhere to. Besides the advice offered up by Hamlet in the play of the same name, everyone from Stella Adler to Stanford Meisner, to Lee Strasberg to Uta Hagen has wisdom to offer. But if you have been a careful reader and student of acting, you have probably noticed that although these approaches have their own specific elements, they share a strong common thread. In fact, if we really looked carefully at all the approaches offered up these days, we would find that they have far more in common than they have differences. That is because, no matter what teacher we study with or what acting book we read, the concepts being discussed come from the basic vocabulary and ideas first introduced by Konstantin Stanislavski, the great Russian director and acting teacher.

Stanislavski spent most of his long artistic life trying to find a tangible technique for actors to use that would parallel the craft available to artists in other art forms. Painters, musicians, dancers, and writers all had such techniques available to them, but until Stanislavski began to develop his own approach to the acting process, actors learned primarily by observing and imitating the actors they worked with and admired, and by getting on the stage and figuring out what to do by doing it. Although it may be true that the trail of great actors extends all the way back to ancient Greece, it is also true that before Stanislavski, very little was written about acting that could prove practically useful if actors wanted to learn how to do what Kean and Forrest and Thespis apparently did so well. Hamlet's speech to the players is, of course, an exception, but it is far shorter and less detailed than the three volumes that the Russian master eventually published.

Stanislavski's research spanned some fifty years, and during that time his theories on acting took shape, expanded, and changed in accordance with what he observed about human behavior, what he learned from his students and coworkers in the studio, and what he discovered while trying to apply his theories to the work he and his fellow players created for performance. These changes are reflected by the differences in his approach to acting expressed in his three published volumes: *The Actor Prepares, Building a Character,* and *Creating the Role.* Stanislavski was never afraid of being wrong or of changing his mind. Throughout his long career he documented his theories in writing and continued to publish his ideas as they developed and changed.

In his early work, the great Russian director believed that the core to truthful, believable acting lay in the actor's ability to find emotional truth through the use of sense memory and substitution. He later came to believe that this kind of focus led an actor to concentrate on the self at the expense of the script and often caused actors to try to repeat effects earlier created rather than being in the moment. In his later work, he turned instead to the theories of physical action, which he came to feel were more reliable, repeatable, learnable, and ultimately more truthful.

It was not until the 1930s, some thirty years after its publication in Russia, that Stanislavski's first book on acting theory was published in English and made its way to American shores. It was immediately embraced by the members of the Group Theatre, one of the most important acting companies in the history of American theatre. Lee Strasberg, one of the company's principal acting teachers and founding directors, was so taken by the book, in fact, that he adapted its content for his own use as a teacher almost immediately.

What he took from Stanislavski's book eventually became known in America as "the Method."

Not all of the Group Theatre was as taken with *An Actor Prepares* as Strasberg was, and this difference of opinion about what acting is and how it should be taught contributed to the eventual dissolution of the company. Stella Adler, Robert Lewis, Harold Clurman, Elia Kazan, and Sanford Meisner, all members of the Group Theatre, eventually, not unlike the twelve tribes of Israel, picked up their tents and wandered away from the Group, ultimately starting acting studios of their own in New York. All of them continued to develop their own theories and approaches to the craft of acting. All of them successfully produced actors of exceptional talent and training, many of whom became famous in film. All of them continued to use the same basic principles first catalogued, described, and explored by Konstantin Stanislavski.

Stanislavski's later work is the source for much of what you have found in this book. It is sometimes known as an outside-in approach to acting. That simply means that the technique starts with an action rather than a feeling, and the presumption is that a strongly played action will generate an appropriate corresponding feeling (commit to kicking a can in a manner that an angry person would, and the action will generate feelings of anger). This particular approach was embraced by Stella Adler and became a central part of her teaching. The Method, as taught by Lee Strasberg, was an inside-out approach. This technique starts with the generation of a truthful emotion that should color the dialogue and physicality that is in turn generated from that truthful feeling. Both techniques have their place, but I share the opinion that the outside-in approach is more accessible and reliable for most actors, especially beginning ones. I also believe that relying on personal emotional truth can lead an actor away from serving the script—dangerous unless an actor is very experienced and very, very talented. For those of you who have not approached your work from the inside-out philosophy, you may want to do so at some time in the future. It can be added into the action-based work you have already done and can complement the analysis you must continue to develop. But no matter what parts of the craft become your most reliable tools, the process of scene study will continue to provide the framework for your growth. I hope this book has helped you on your journey.

GLOSSARY OF ACTING TERMS

Since it is essential that actors be familiar with all the jargon of the craft and understand the concepts and application those terms suggest, here follows in alphabetical order a partial list of acting terms and definitions that are most often used today. Each term has worked its way permanently into the lexicon of acting and each concept, into the actor's toolbox of technique. Some words have been bent or twisted since their first introduction by Stanislavski, others may have evolved into something seemingly different, and still others may seem to be inventions of an era that came long after Stanislavski's exit into the wings. But each of these terms, whether newly minted or antique, owes at least something to the Russian teacher and director who began the development of acting craft as we know it today.

ACTING

The most common definition I have seen for *acting* goes something like this: "behaving believably under fictional circumstances." And that certainly describes the process. However, a more useful definition—one that I have come to employ over the years—might be the one that defines *good* acting. It goes something like this: "acting that is believable and that tells the best possible story while serving the script." All actors, of course, must be believable. The audience must accept an actor's work as he or she moves through the world of the play in a step-by-step sequence of action. *Believable* is not synonymous with *realistic*, however. A nonrealistic play may require choices that are not necessarily realistic but are consistent with the universe created by the playwright. The actor wants to tell the best possible story, as well—one that is the most interesting he or she can possibly create. That story, however, must be consistent with the intentions of the playwright and the production. Hugely entertaining choices for a character cannot be considered good acting choices if they are inconsistent with the overall needs of the play. Each actor must make choices that contribute to the overall whole of the play and, like a piece of a jigsaw puzzle, must fit perfectly with the surrounding pieces.

ACTION

Action has several meanings pertinent to the acting process. *Action* can refer to the cause-and-effect sequence of events in a play—essential for understanding the given plot and for making choices that are consistent with and supportive of that plot. This kind of action can also be referred to as the *throughline* or **arc**. The term *action* can also apply to any physical or psychological activity an actor carries out in the course of the play, as in "What is the action you are playing?" This kind of action is more frequently called an actor's **objective** or *intention*. It is important to keep in mind that no matter which of these definitions is being employed, action is an essential ingredient of drama and closely related to the dramatic engine of all drama: conflict. Actors who focus on emotion or character, rather than on action, are in danger of falling into theatrical quicksand—for, as Stanislavski came to believe, actions are doable; playing emotion or character directly is less so. (See also **Physical Action.**)

ADLER, STELLA

Stella Adler was a member of one of the most famous acting families in America and one of the original members of the Group Theatre who challenged Lee Strasberg's interpretations of the Stanislavski system. She later went to Paris and studied with the Russian master herself. Upon her return, she explained Stanislavski's most recent theories of acting, which focused on physical action, to the Group Theatre. Lee Strasberg rejected these ideas and began referring to Stanislavski's earlier emotional work as "the Method," the technique he later became universally famous for. Adler, too, went on to become one of America's foremost acting teachers, focusing on physical and psychological action, imagination, and the use of the script.

ANALYSIS AND SYNTHESIS

Analysis and *synthesis* are the intellectual tools necessary for breaking down a script and putting it back together so that it will work effectively for an audience. Good acting begins with an understanding of the play and the ability to make acting choices that serve that understanding. Contrary to the beliefs of some, acting is not simply about actors being able to personalize their feeling onto a script, but rather about communicating what characters think and feel to an audience so that the audience will understand the story of the play as written by the playwright—the story crafted by the combined choices of actors and directors to be as compelling and clear as possible.

ARC

Also known as the **action** or *throughline,* the arc is the journey each character makes through the course of a scene or play, or it is the sequential action of the play overall. It is essential that actors recognize and respond to each of the sequential events of the play and make choices that demonstrate how these events affect and alter their characters. The bigger the arc, the greater the journey, and the more the character changes during the course of the play. In general, the bigger the difference between the character at the end of the play and at the beginning, the more interesting the performance, and the more interesting the play—provided the audience sees the actor making those changes as the character. It is up to the actors to understand the journey made by their characters and to communicate them through their chosen actions.

BEAT

A *beat* is the length of script during which an actor plays a particular objective, tactic, or action. A beat is always preceded by a transition and followed by another. The term, coined by Stanislavski, is actually the result of a mispronunciation of the English word "bit" with a Russian accent, although there is a logic to the word *beat,* as well. A particular beat (recognizable pattern or rhythm) is played until a victory, defeat, discovery, or new information causes the beat to end. When this occurs, there is a transition, at which point a new beat is established and played. As Stanislavski probably originally meant it, one bit (or small section of action) is followed by another and another, creating the throughline of the scene.

BEGINNINGS, MIDDLES, AND ENDS

Beginnings, middles, and *ends* are the necessary steps that an actor must go through for all effective storytelling. Plays, scenes, beats, and even moments have beginnings, middles, and ends. So do all physical actions. Actors who fail to find the beginnings, middles, and ends to actions, moments, or any other aspects of their work will fail to be believable and will fail to execute choices that are clear and compelling for an audience. Most actions, for instance, start with the reason for the action. Actors who ignore this origin jump into a middle and fail to communicate believably the story sequence they are undertaking. Dialogue, for instance, doesn't begin with the first word. It begins with the need to speak. Beginning actors doing a monologue often begin with the words rather than the need to speak. It often takes them several moments before they connect with what they are saying, so that the words have been wasted and the actor looks bad. Here is another example. Try yawning. If you started with opening your mouth, you probably failed to execute a believable yawn. Yawns start with the impulse to yawn. So does an acting moment. The yawn is complete not when the physical action of yawning is complete, but when the result that the yawn produces in the yawner is apparent to the yawner and to the audience. Only when the beginnings, middles, and ends are fully executed is the storytelling potential realized.

BLOCKING

Blocking concerns the physical elements of storytelling onstage—movement, gestures, and business. Actors often expect that the director will provide them with their blocking in rehearsals. But as Stanislavski came to believe, the physical choices made by actors are as much a part of the acting as delivering the lines is. The physical actions executed by actors can tell as much about their characters and about the story as any other acting tool at the performer's disposal. Actors who can act with their bodies as well as with their voices, with or without the director's input, are better actors for the ability. Physical action, as Stanislavski came to believe, can connect actors with their truthful emotional center. But even without that connection, actors who can communicate thought and emotion to an audience through what they physically do are the strongest at their craft.

BUSINESS

Business is any ongoing physical activity an actor carries out while pursuing or completing an acting objective onstage. Smoking or drinking are examples of stage business that can add to the actor's characterization and believability, by giving details of the character being played through the manner in which he smokes or drinks. Business is almost always secondary to the main action of the scene and objective of the actor. Like driving a car, business can be executed without direct focusing, unless, of course, the business requires focus for a particular moment—lighting the cigarette, for instance. The specifics of the particular business, however, can help shape a moment or inform an audience what a character is thinking or feeling. If I choose to drag on my cigarette after being told that my wife has left me, it gives the audience information. The good actor uses business in a specific way to help shape the performance.

CHARACTER

Character is one of Aristotle's basic elements of drama. Other elements include dialogue, action, idea, spectacle, and music. We often hear actors talking about "being their characters," "inhabiting their characters," and so on. We also hear about creating biographies of characters' lives before and after the action of the play. All this can be dangerous, especially to a beginning actor. Inhabiting character and living out imaginary biographies can lead actors away from fulfilling their responsibilities to tell the story of the play by making acting choices for their characters that come from the script. Besides, becoming a character may be an illusion or impossible for some actors to accomplish. Better to focus on the actions of each character and the manner in which those actions are performed. Character is action, so when combined with externals like costume and makeup, actions go a long way toward becoming character.

CHOICES

All actors must make choices about what their character needs from the other characters who surround them, and choices about the tactics employed to get those needs fulfilled. In real life people seldom think specifically about what they need, or, for that matter, about why they play out many of their actions during the course of the day. Actors, however, must make choices for the characters they play, choices that get them closer to what their characters need, even if the characters themselves are unaware of why they do the things they do. When actors make choices that are seemingly too simple, ones that will get them nearer to their goal, they are invariably serving the built-in conflict of the plot. Any necessary complexity of character will be provided by the script and the audience's perception of character as they watch the action of the play. **Positive** choices are choices that help a character get what she needs. *Negative* choices are choices that do not do so. Actors should play only positive choices. Negative choices make for indulgent and often dull acting—because they diminish or destroy the potential conflict built into a scene by the playwright. Actors should not play their pain. They should acknowledge it and then make new choices that help their character get what they need (fulfill their objectives).

CONFLICT

When two opposing forces meet, *conflict* ensues; conflict is the engine of all drama, and it is the core ingredient an actor must recognize before choosing an objective. Playwrights want to tell the best story they possibly can. They know that the good story centers on a conflict—usually between a central character and the obstacles that character faces. Since that is the way plays are structured, actors must be able to recognize the conflict where it exists and make choices that contribute to that dramatic engine. When actors recognize the conflict in a scene and make their objective relate to another character who will be opposing its fulfillment, they are contributing to the conflict and to the dramatic success of the scene. Scene by scene, this approach almost guarantees an exciting, watchable story.

CRAFT

Craft concerns the tools of acting that can be learned and mastered, unlike talent, which is innate and cannot be learned. The mastery of craft can help gifted actors hone and shape their work. For those less talented, it can go a long way toward substituting for the lack of natural gifts. Those who choose not to master craft will always have to gamble that their instincts are never wrong and constantly be at the mercy of those who seem to have control of the acting situation. Good directors—directors who are focused on and able to bring out the best in each actor—are hard to find. Actors who have mastered craft need rely only on themselves to produce work that gets the job done.

CRITICISM

Criticism is a necessary part of an actor's work. Without an outside eye to bring critical observation, the actor cannot improve the work she offers. Actors who see or feel criticism as negative will have trouble enjoying the creative process and are likely to be difficult to work with. Criticism must be seen as a necessary and positive step toward making the final product the best it can be. Actors who cannot accept criticism naturally must learn to do so quickly. It must be considered part of the craft.

DEFEATS

(See Moments.)

DISCOVERIES

(See Moments.)

EMOTIONAL MEMORY

Emotional memory refers to the use of personal memory to create an emotion that can be used in an acting situation. This internal approach to acting was discovered and employed by Stanislavski in his early work and described in *An Actor Prepares.* He later abandoned this technique in favor of the external physical approach toward acting he wrote about in his later work. Method acting as described and taught by Lee Strasberg relied heavily on emotional memory—the application of real and honest emotions recalled from past experience and applied to the immediate acting situation.

EMOTIONAL TRUTH

Emotional truth comes from actors who can find and produce honest emotions within themselves, emotion that serves the acting situation they are engaged in. At one point Stanislavski felt that emotional truth was best found through the application of emotional memory. He later came to feel that emotional truth could better be found and repeated as a by-product of physical action. Today, most actors accept the validity of both approaches. (See also Emotional Memory.)

ENDOWMENT

Endowment is giving an object specific emotional meaning that can be effectively used for acting purposes. Every prop an actor uses has potential for creating wonderful acting moments that can help communicate how the character is feeling or what she is thinking. When Dorothy first picks up the ruby slipper, left by the late witch of the east, she does not simply pick it up. She endows the object with the emotion of the moment. When her three friends receive their worthless gifts from the wizard, each endows the objects received with what those objects mean to them, thereby creating wonderful acting moments lasting only seconds onscreen, but staying with the audience for the rest of their lives.

EXTERNAL AND INTERNAL

(See Emotional Truth and Physical Action.)

GENRE

Genre refers to the kind of play the author has written, such as drama, comedy, farce, tragedy. Each type of play has certain characteristics that must be acknowledged and adhered to and may even require a particular style of acting if the play is to be acted effectively. A modern comedy, for instance, is expected to be funny, so the actor must make choices that support the playwright's intention. The actor must try to add to what the playwright has provided and certainly must never diminish what the playwright has offered up as the starting point.

GESTURE

A *gesture* is a single specific physical action that communicates emotion, information, or attitude. A choice in a moment of the play to take your hand and place it on your forehead after hearing that your daughter has died is a gesture. Shaking a fisted hand at an adversary after being embarrassed by him is also a gesture. Each communicates, through its simple execution, information and emotion about the character being played and about the thoughts and feelings of that character. Gestures can be calculated, planned choices that through the rehearsal process become natural and organic, or they may be discovered spontaneously as they happen during the rehearsal process or in performance and, because they work, be adopted as part of the performance and used again and again by the actor at that particular moment of the play.

GIVEN CIRCUMSTANCES

Given circumstances are the who, what, where, and when of a play or scene that must be considered before making acting choices. When a line from a play is delivered and makes sense in terms of the context of the play, an audience gives it little thought. "Of course, that's the way it should be said," our subconscious would tell us, were we to ask it. It is only when we ask a nonactor to say a particular line that we realize any line of dialogue can be said in literally an infinite number of ways. Which way is right? Which best serves the play? Which best serves the character saying it? Examining the given circumstances of the play, the scene, and the moment helps the actor narrow down the choices. The four *W*s refer to the *who*, the character saying the line; the *what*, the situation in which she finds herself; the *where*, the location in which this occurs; and the *when*, the time both general and specific of the occurrence. Take the line "I love you." How many ways can the line be said? Now narrow down the choices by manipulating the given circumstances. The number remains vast, but you are no longer operating in the dark.

INDICATING

When a performer physically demonstrates an action without personal connection to what she is supposed to be thinking, feeling, or doing, she is indicating rather than fully committing to the action.

INTENTION

(See Objective.)

JOURNEY

(See Action and Arc.)

JUSTIFICATION

Justification is the process an actor goes through to make sure that a line or moment is acted in such a way that it is both believable and clear, and makes sense in terms of the given circumstances of the situation. A line that is not justified will sound wrong or empty when delivered in the context of the play. It will sound like the actor is simply saying the line rather than having a need or purpose for saying it. A playwright has reasons for everything she puts into a script. An actor must discover those reasons and use them to support or enhance what is on the printed page or implied by it.

LISTENING

Listening is a basic requirement for an actor if she is to be believed, and an essential step for staying in the moment and reacting effectively. Actors who do not listen may be reliable performers, but their work never varies, seldom grows, and almost never presents the audience or fellow actors the gift of spontaneity that being in the moment brings. Being able to adjust to the nuances of each performance keeps an actor's work fresh and alive, and the magic found by simply being able to listen and respond to all that is happening in a freshly created moment is the ingredient that can make some actors' work so real and exciting. Those who simply wait their turn to say a line are easily distinguishable from the good actor. So important is the skill of listening that Sanford Meisner devoted most of his teaching time to developing this aspect of his students' craft. (See also **Meisner, Sanford**.)

MAGIC IF, THE

The magic if is an acting term coined by Stanislavski that reminds an actor to ask, "What would I do if I were this character in this situation?" Notice that the question states *do,* not *feel.* Because Stanislavski came to believe that playing out the appropriate actions told the audience more about the character's feelings and thoughts than working with emotion directly, his "magic if" became an essential tool. Here is an example. Say you are Laura from *The Glass Menagerie.* You have just been told by Tom, your brother, that your mother, Amanda, has died. What do you do? Act it now. You may be stuck, especially if you simply try to conjure up some emotional response. But what we know about Laura can give us some good starting clues to actions she might take, which in turn could provide the actor with a springboard for her emotional response. Perhaps Laura would go toward her menagerie to find some comfort. Perhaps she would pick up some pieces and examine them closely. Perhaps she would stroke her favorite or hold it tightly in her palm while putting it next to her cheek. Character and story can be communicated through what we do and how we do it. Asking the "magic if" can help lead us to those choices.

MEISNER, SANFORD

Sanford Meisner was one of the great first generation of acting teachers that came from the Group Theatre. Meisner devoted much of his teaching time to finding techniques to better enable his students to listen well and stay in the moment. His most famous exercises are used by countless acting students around the world, whatever approach to acting they are studying. The Meisner repetition games, in which actors repeat what their acting partners say to them and try to turn these repetitions into actual conversations, have become a standard practice that is highly valued by all who teach and study acting.

METHOD, THE

The Method is an internal approach to acting centering on the use of emotional truth and sense memory, made famous by Lee Strasberg but based primarily on early writings of Stanislavski. Critics of this approach, such as Stella Adler, felt the Method was self-indulgent and often made actors look good at the expense of the play. But even she would probably agree that the Method was a highly effective technique for film acting, in which only a moment might be shot at a time and the intimacy of the camera demanded an emotional presence and honesty not necessarily required by stage acting.

MOMENT

A moment is the smallest unit of dramatic action that can be acted. While in rehearsal and performance, actors must learn through effective analytical reading and good listening where moments occur and pick up on the execution of them. Every created moment is an important contribution to the overall story and to the story of each individual character. A fully realized moment has to be clear and full and most often has a beginning, middle, and end. Moments can occur at any justified time but most often occur at the end of a beat following the delivery of new information, when a discovery is made, or when there is a victory or a defeat in terms of the actor's objective. Any new information an actor as character learns should be reacted to. Examples from *The Glass Menagerie* include when Amanda learns that Tom is planning to leave, or when Laura learns that her mother knows she has not been attending business school. Examples of a discovery are when Olivia realizes why she has been given a ring from the Duke in *Twelfth Night*, or, in *As You Like It*, when Rosalind (disguised as a man) realizes that Phoebe is in love with her. Victories are the actable moments when objectives are reached. When Tom wins the argument about his leaving home and Amanda accepts the fact, it is a moment (although followed by a transition during which Amanda comes up with a new strategy and new plan of attack.) Or when Jim convinces Laura to join him on the floor of the living room, thereby breaking through her wall of resistance, that is a moment of victory, as well. Those same moments are defeats for Amanda and Jim respectively, and the actors playing them have and should take the opportunity to respond in those moments. These kinds of moments are often followed by moments of transition—equally interesting and equally important to act. (See Transitions.)

MOMENT TO MOMENT

Moment to moment refers to the ability of the good actor to respond to what an acting partner is saying and doing at a particular moment. Moment-to-moment acting requires good listening and is essential for believability, spontaneity, and the discovery of actions that can define a moment.

MOTIVATION

Motivation is the reason behind a character pursuing a particular objective. Motivation cannot be played directly but can be used as a device to find the acting objective that can and must be played at every moment of a character's stage life. Here is an example: I am jealous of my brother. My mother always liked him better. How do I play jealous? I cannot. But I can try to hurt him whenever possible—to get back at him for taking all our mother's love. Jealousy is the motivation; punishing my brother is my objective. I can and should play my objective.

MOVEMENT

Movement is an aspect of blocking—when an actor travels from one place to another onstage. An actor should never perform purposeless movement. An actor crosses the stage because his character needs to put distance between himself and another character, or because he needs to cut down the distance between them. If an actor chooses to move away from someone or something, he is also moving toward someone or something else—with purpose. These movements have beginnings, middles, and ends, and the character should carry out these steps onstage to help him communicate his thoughts and feelings. Any movement should be connected to the actor's particular objective at any given time onstage. Since physical positioning can help a character get what he needs or keep another character from getting what she needs, the physical relationship between characters onstage should be used to establish or maintain power and weakness that tie into a character's objective. The good actor is aware of this physical dynamic and uses this tool to pursue his purpose and help reveal his inner life to the watching audience.

NEGATIVE CHOICES

(See Choices.)

NEW INFORMATION

(See Choices.)

OBJECTIVES

Objectives are he needs an actor playing a character must pursue at all times onstage. Acting is not the same as life; it just closely resembles it when well done. No matter how well the actor probes the psyche and emotions of a character from the printed page, to some extent the actor is pretending. His words are not his or her own; they are borrowed from the playwright who has written them for just this purpose. In life a person's actions are often random, and where they will lead, a person never fully knows until they are played out. Life is messy, often leaving many loose ends. A character in a play, on the other hand, is a creation resulting from the imagination of a playwright with the power to select and control the actions of that character so that they play out in accordance with the action of the play being written. It follows, then, that a character's behavior is simpler by far than that of a living, breathing person. Each choice, each action the actor-as-character chooses and plays must therefore support the track the playwright has laid out. By pursuing the goal of the character, whether the character is aware of that goal or not, the actor creates the illusion of reality while making choices that ultimately serve the story of the character and of the play. Most objectives should be connected to the other characters who share a scene. Chances are that if a playwright put two characters in a scene, the conflict lies between those characters. The objective—to win something from that other character—most often arises from this conflict.

OBSTACLES

Obstacles are the elements in a scene or play that keep a character from obtaining his or her objective. They provide conflict and heighten the stakes of any acting situation. These obstacles can be in the form of another character (Tybalt for Romeo). They can be internal (the struggle in Friar Lawrence to decide whether he should perform the marriage rites for Romeo and Juliet or not). They can be external (the politics of Nazi Germany that infuses *The Diary of Anne Frank*). Or they can be inanimate (the weather in *The Grapes of Wrath*). Whatever the category, obstacles help keep the actions of a character and the overall story of a play interesting and exciting. Ask yourself what obstacles Laura in *The Glass Menagerie* faces—internally, from another character, and as a result of the given circumstances of the play. Now do the same for Tom, Amanda, and the "gentleman caller." Notice how these obstacles make both the characters and the story more interesting. Actors must look for these obstacles in the script and use them to make their journey through the story as exciting as possible.

PHYSICAL ACTION

Physical action consists of the tangible and visible things a character does onstage. Try playing anger directly. Take a moment now and try to conjure anger. Did you feel it? Would I recognize this feeling were I an audience watching? Now make a fist and slam it on a table as though you were angry. Did you fully commit to the action? If you did, you probably felt anger. The audience watching probably would have recognized your action as anger, as well. Now plan a sequence of actions that tells a story and that communicates what you are thinking and feeling. Make your physical planning specific, and rehearse each action carefully in sequence. When you have done so, you are acting in the manner that Stanislavski describes in his later work. This kind of approach to acting is clear, interesting, controllable, and repeatable. So is the good actor's work.

POSITIVE CHOICES

(See Choices.)

PSYCHOLOGICAL ACTION

(See Action.)

RISK

Risk is a basic tool for producing interesting acting; the more risk taken, the more interesting the actor in a situation. Another term for this concept is *the big choice*. What makes you the more interesting actor—simply doing what is believable, or making the most interesting believable choice possible? The actor who takes risks and does so in a believable manner is the one who get jobs—because she is the one who produces the most watchable work. The acting moments best remembered are the ones in which the actor surprises you, yet you recognize the rightness of the choice.

SENSE MEMORY

The use of personal memory relating to smell, sound, taste, touch, and sight to enhance the emotional power of an acting moment or situation. The actor who must smell the imaginary flower onstage will enhance his work by recalling specifically the beautiful fragrance of a flower actually smelled. Sense memories are among the strongest we possess. We can often remember the moment we actually heard a song for the first time, the dinnertime smell of the house we grew up in, the taste of the first lobster we ever ate. Actors must make real for themselves all that they do onstage and find ways to communicate those things to an audience. By leading themselves to precise moments in such memories of sense, they can apply what they discover to the current acting work.

STAKES

What is at risk for the actor-as-character as she pursues her objective? These discovered *stakes* can help the actor make the acting situation as interesting as possible. As Amanda pressures Tom to bring home a suitor for Laura (*The Glass Menagerie*), what is at risk for her? As Laura comes out of her shell to meet the expectation and pressure of her gentleman caller, what does she risk?

When Romeo climbs the orchard wall or when Juliet agrees to meet her new lover at Friar Lawrence's cell, what is each risking? In all of these cases, the characters are willing to chance an enormous amount in order to get what they want. Awareness of what is at stake keeps the danger factor high for actors and tells the audience quite a bit about the characters they are playing. Finding the stakes in less obviously risky situations is a more difficult trick. But since plays tell stories filled with conflict, the playwright has stuffed them with huge risk potential. It is up to the actor to find the high stakes and use them to make the work as exciting as possible.

STANISLAVSKI, KONSTANTIN

Konstantin Stanislavski is the Russian theatre director, actor, and teacher responsible for most of the basic craft used in actor training. (See also the chapter "Final Notes," as well as the introduction to this glossary.)

STRASBERG, LEE

The most famous of the great seminal American acting teachers, Lee Strasberg developed "the Method," employed by many of the great realistic film actors of the postwar era. (See also the introduction to this glossary; see also **the Method**.)

STYLE

Simply put, *style* is the world of the play. Actors must know the world of the play in which they are performing and make choices in thought and action that are consistent with those of the other actors in the play and with the world created by the playwright. *Realism,* for instance, though referred to as an acting style, really refers to the kind of world created by the playwright—a world that seems very much like the one we inhabit in our own contemporary life. The American plays of the 1930s, plays such as *Awake and Sing!,* were examples of realism in the time they were written. Today, their language no longer represents what we consider realism. But they present a consistent world throughout. The actor must understand and find a way to act believably within a given world.

SUBSTITUTION

Substitution is a technique in which an actor substitutes a parallel personal memory from his own life for a similar one in the play he is working on to enhance his emotional connection to a moment. Often used by Strasberg in his Method approach to acting, although he later abandoned its use. Stella Adler found substitution to be a ridiculously distracting approach to an acting problem because it separated the actor from being in the moment of the play. (See also **Stella Adler; Method, the;** and **Lee Strasberg.**)

TACTICS

Tactics are the specific strategies an actor-as-character uses while pursuing her objective. Some acting teachers break objectives down into smaller units when analyzing a script, and these are usually referred to as *tactics.* For instance, your objective is to get your father to let you use the car tonight. He is against the idea. How many approaches can you come up with to get the car before your father finally gives in to you? Make a list of your strategies. Those are your tactics. You use them one at a time until you accomplish your objective and get your father to put the keys in your hand. In a scene, an actor as character often goes through the same process, whether planned or spontaneously. Each strategy is a tactic employed until there is a recognition that the tactic has succeeded or failed, at which time another and another is thought up and employed until the objective is fulfilled or abandoned.

THROUGHLINE

(See Arc.)

TRANSITIONS

Transitions are the actable moments when one objective is given up and replaced with another. This transition occurs as a result of an objective being lost, won, or abandoned because of new information, an interruption, or a discovery. Often the transitional moment provides the actor with a wonderful opportunity to show the audience what she is thinking or feeling. Sometimes, however, the rapid switch to a new tactic or objective without hesitation can be extremely interesting, as well, but only if the audience understands the jump. Here are some examples. You have been pressuring your father for the keys to his car. He gives them to you—a **victory** moment is played followed by the finding of a new objective, to get him to give you gas money. Your father threatens that if you say one thing more on the subject of car keys he will ground you for a month—a **defeat**. While you are sweet-talking your father, there is a phone call for you and you find out that Billy got his dad's car for the evening—**new information** that changes the situation. During your tactical advance on Dad, your mother enters with news that Aunt Joan has been in a car accident—an **interruption** and new information that changes the situation completely. While Dad is denying your advances, he is very funny and charming. You realize that you would rather stay home with the family than go out—a **discovery** that forces you into a transitional moment.

VICTORIES

(See Moments.)